FIND ME A ROCKSTAR

FIND ME A ROCKSTAR

How Top Companies

Win the Talent War

RITA BAROODY

FIND ME A ROCKSTAR
How Top Companies Win the Talent War

Published by **Selective Insight**
www.selectiveinsight.com

ISBN 979-8-9940367-0-9

For my daughter Ava—may this book remind you that your success is defined not just by what you achieve but by who you inspire along the way.

CONTENTS

FOREWORD

Building a high-performing team is about more than just technical skills. It requires chemistry, communication, mental agility, humility, and ambition from each individual—and that's the standards we adhere to at The Siegfried Group.

In *Find Me a Rockstar*, I was struck by how closely Rita's philosophy aligns with what we hold in our own organization. Her emphasis on prioritizing intangible qualities reflects the very approach we've long taken in our interviews and hiring decisions. Rather than focusing solely on resumes and technical skills, we've always believed that the true measure of a candidate lies in their character, adaptability, and alignment with our culture.

Reading Rita's book felt like a validation of these principles. She articulates, with clarity and conviction, why quality should always come before quantity in recruiting. Too often, agencies flood us with resumes that check the boxes but miss the mark on what really matters. Rita understands that the best hires are those who elevate the team, drive momentum, and embody the values that make an organization thrive.

Rita's insights and teachings included go beyond theory to provide actionable frameworks and real-world stories that resonate with anyone who's ever faced the challenge of building a high-performing team. The Build–Engage–Close™ model is practical, insightful, and refreshingly honest about the complexities of finding and keeping top talent.

For leaders who believe that people are the greatest asset—and that the right people are the ultimate multiplier—this book is both a guide and a source of inspiration. Rita's perspective is a welcome addition to the conversation about what truly defines excellence in recruiting.

Jeff Osberg
Senior Vice President,
National Markets & Sales Team
The Siegfried Group, LLP

WHY I WROTE THIS BOOK

I've sat on both sides of the hiring table as an executive recruiter trusted to deliver consistent results and as a business leader making high-stakes talent decisions.

What I've seen time and again is that when the right people *align* with the right vision, everything accelerates.

My passion lies in alignment: aligning talent with vision, and vision with execution, so companies can grow faster, stronger, and smarter.

But that alignment doesn't happen by chance.

Too often, companies miss out on top talent because they rely on outdated strategies, unclear positioning, or the wrong people leading the hiring process. At the same time, exceptional professionals are overlooked, not because they lack ability, but because the system wasn't built to reveal their value.

That disconnect is costly. It slows growth, weakens culture, and erodes long-term value.

I wrote this book because I've seen the transformation that happens when companies get it *right,* and I believe far more can.

This is for strategic, growth-minded leaders who know that talent isn't just about headcount. It is your greatest competitive advantage.

And the right rockstars do more than just support your vision, they scale it. Let's find them.

PART I

BUILD

CHAPTER 1

ROCKSTARS DON'T GROW ON TREES

What's the cost of one wrong hire?

It's more than financial. It's lost momentum, diminished morale, and millions in long-term value. Every great leader knows the future of their business depends on one thing: the ability to secure high-performing talent. And yet even the most admired companies often get it wrong. Not because they lack reputation or resources but because hiring top talent takes more than instinct or luck. It takes the right strategy.

Research from McKinsey shows that companies who put talent at the center of their strategy are 4.2x more likely to outperform competitors, with revenue growth averaging 30% higher than their peers.[1]

As the war for talent escalates, the shortage of top performers has become a strategic risk.

As industrial titan Henry Ford once said, "You can take my factories, burn up my buildings, but give me my people and I'll build the business right back again." But you don't need to dive into history to know that attracting and retaining the right people is what separates good companies from great ones. Still, it is the one area that companies struggle with the most.

Why is that? It should be simple, right?

You have an exceptional company that people want to work for. You just need to find them, hire them, and work happily ever after. What most organizations miss are the critical, nuanced action steps required at each stage in the recruitment process to make that possible, especially when you are targeting *top* talent.

This book isn't about hiring warm bodies or filling roles. It's about securing **rockstars**—the *rare* professionals who elevate everything they touch. These individuals don't need managing. They don't miss details. They drive profitability, sharpen execution, and raise the performance bar for everyone around them. They spot what others overlook, act with ownership, and move the business forward in measurable ways.

Rockstars are not easy to find.

They're not easy to win.

And they don't grow on trees.

But when you do find and win rockstars, they become force multipliers inside your organization. And that's what this book is about—building the strategy to find them, win them, and keep them.

Transformative Strategy

Early on in my strategic recruitment firm, *Selective Insight*, I partnered with a private equity-backed hospitality company we'll call "Hardworking Hospitality" (to protect confidentiality). The PE firm behind them, "Plenty of PE," had a diverse portfolio, including a recruiting agency we'll call "Regular Recruiting."

For years, Plenty of PE encouraged all of its portfolio companies, including Hardworking Hospitality, to use Regular Recruiting. The logic was simple. It would benefit the ecosystem of companies they owned or invested in. But what they failed to realize was that Regular Recruiting lacked both a network of high performers and the strategic approach required to attract high-caliber talent.

Over time, the CFO of Hardworking Hospitality was becoming increasingly frustrated with the limitations of Regular Recruiting. They were sending him candidates, yes, but they were pushing *high* quantity and *low* quality. The recruiters didn't understand the strategic roles they were filling, and as a result, they were unable to accurately articulate the opportunities to candidates.

Regular Recruiting was actually making the CFO's job harder. And while on the surface, it seemed financially sound to use a recruiting firm from within the same PE portfolio, in reality, Hardworking Hospitality suffered from poor performance and high turnover from the hires—revealing that short-term savings came at the expense of long-term success. What looked efficient on paper turned out to be costly in execution. It was a transactional relationship with no strategic upside.

The breaking point came when a VP Finance candidate placed by Regular Recruiting failed to analyze the company's financials accurately and didn't take the necessary action steps to save the company money. That one hire cost Hardworking Hospitality **an estimated $2 million in missed cost savings** by overlooking supply chain, inventory, insurance, and procurement inefficiencies.

Even worse, the hire failed to improve cash flow visibility, restructure underperforming cost centers, and failed to accurately deliver the strategic insights the board was expecting. Hardworking

Hospitality quickly realized they had not secured a top performer—they had settled for a seat filler.

While the immediate loss was significant, the true cost was far greater. When you factor in operational drag, lost momentum, team disruption, and delayed valuation growth, the total impact was easily up to **ten times that**—a **$20 million mistake** hiding behind a single bad hire.

It wasn't just a bad hire. It was a missed opportunity to create measurable enterprise value.

Hardworking Hospitality was looking to flip the company in the next three to five years. That loss lowered their bottom line and therefore decreased their valuation and attractiveness to buyers. It was a massive error with serious consequences. And it was the final straw for the CFO, whose own job was now on the line, because his board members felt the responsibility landed with *him*. He knew there was a gap in the quality of talent being presented to him—and he needed a better solution.

I was introduced to this CFO through a trusted, mutual friend, who also happened to be another one of my clients. Our mutual connection contacted me and said, "I know someone who needs your help. Can I put you in touch?"

We met in-person at his office, and he started off explaining the pain points of his company's current recruiting service. "I am supposed to leverage Regular Recruiting, but there is nothing to leverage," he told me. "Of course, we want to stay in our PE space. But this recruiter is not a good strategic partner. They don't even understand how our finance function operates, so how can they understand the positions we need to fill? I tell them what I'm looking for, and they keep giving me candidates who are completely misaligned with the role and our vision. Frankly, they are introducing me to professionals who are unimpressive."

There was *no* alignment with Regular Recruiting and Hardworking Hospitality—aside from the fact that they were both backed by Plenty of PE. That lack of alignment extended to the candidates being presented and resulted in wasted time and energy.

Even though Regular Recruiting specialized in accounting and finance, they lacked strategic insight and the ability to align top talent. They couldn't attract high performers because they were not high performers themselves.

Like attracts like—a core principle in strategic recruitment that we will further discuss in this book (more details in Chapter 2). If the recruitment process isn't attracting high performers, it's likely because the recruiters themselves aren't aligned with the caliber of talent you need. Just because a recruiter specializes in a function doesn't mean they specialize in attracting rockstars.

What I saw here was that the CFO was being pushed to leverage the *wrong* recruiting partner, which happens quite frequently with private equity firms and other organizations where procurement restricts the vendor list. Too often, these decisions are made based on outdated criteria such as vendor status, price, or perceived efficiency—rather than capability, strategic fit, or results. It was a bad fit, and more importantly, it was impacting his bottom line and costing him time, money, and unnecessary stress.

With my background in finance and accounting, along with my experience as a CPA, I identified the issues immediately, and he was able to trust my advice. I presented a strategic plan for recruiting high performers and walked him through my **Build–Engage–Close™ Framework**. And one of the red flags I highlighted to him was the disconnect between what his company needed to increase their bottom line and the pressure that Plenty of PE was putting on him to simply increase the headcount. They were pushing for "bodies" in seats, when they would accomplish much more with one or two high-performing professionals who were committed, aligned, and would drive their ROI.

When I told him this, he lit up. He said, "You know, no one else is telling me this, but that is exactly what we need."

I walked him through my process for attracting and vetting top talent, then sent him three high-performing candidates. Two were hired, due in large part to my firm's commitment to consistently prioritizing *quality over quantity*. They adapted quickly and delivered results in a short period of time. Unlike the hires from Regular Recruiting, our candidates all had a proven track record of success, strong leadership qualities, and most importantly, were **culturally aligned**. They hit the ground running, made the CFO's life easier, and helped lead the company to a successful, highly profitable exit transaction.

"We're getting spoiled by you," he said to me on one of our calls. "I wish I'd started working with you sooner."

The right people make all the difference. Or as business guru Jim Collins put it, "People are not your most important asset. The *right* people are."

The right strategic recruiter doesn't just fill roles—they help you assess who is the right hire and they introduce rockstars who can truly transform your organization. They have your company's best interest at heart. That's real partnership, and it is invaluable to the growth and success of every business.

*"People are not your most important asset.
The* **right** *people are."*

– Jim Collins

The Build–Engage–Close Framework

The wrong hire doesn't just underperform—they drag down everything you've worked to build. Low performers drain time, energy, and resources, and worst of all, they demotivate the high-performing team members around them. There is a well-known saying in computer science, "Garbage in, garbage out," meaning that flawed or poor-quality information is destined to result in poor-quality results, and the same holds true in recruitment. You do not want bad hires or a transactional recruiter to ruin performance, inhibit growth, or negatively impact your own career and company's success.

In this book, I'll show you how to strategically win top talent by focusing on quality over quantity, protecting your brand and values, and avoiding costly hiring mistakes.

You'll also be introduced to my **Build–Engage–Close Framework**, a proven methodology designed to help growth-minded leaders like yourself strategically attract, vet, and retain top talent aligned with your long-term business goals.

Build–Engage–Close™ Framework

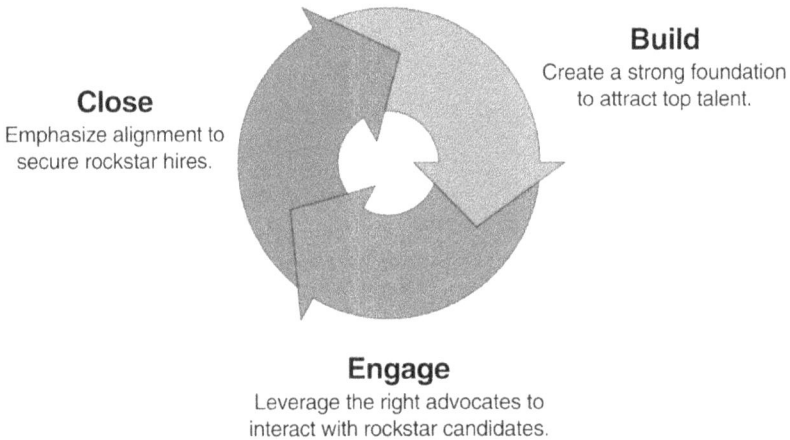

Build
Create a strong foundation
to attract top talent.

Close
Emphasize alignment to
secure rockstar hires.

Engage
Leverage the right advocates to
interact with rockstar candidates.

Every company—and even the best leaders—have blind spots. My framework is designed to help you identify critical gaps and to fully optimize your entire recruitment strategy, driving long-term growth and retention of rockstar talent.

It starts with **building** a strong foundation rooted in a high-performing culture and compelling brand. This foundation creates a "**Rockstar Attraction Engine**" that organically draws high performers to your organization, instead of having to chase them.

Then, we move to **engaging** rockstar candidates using specific, proven techniques—including innovative sales tactics tailored for recruitment, strategies for assessing alignment, and advanced vetting and interviewing methods to ensure they're the right fit.

Finally, the framework guides you in **closing** high performers, from how to extend an offer the right way so that they don't choose your competitor, how to handle negotiations, and what to do after an offer is accepted to maximize retention of your rockstar hires.

Top performers are 400% more productive than average employees, and in highly complex roles, the gap can reach 800%.

Leveraging the Build–Engage–Close Framework will give you a new edge and transform your approach to recruitment. Research consistently shows that top performers deliver substantially greater output and impact compared to average employees. A study cited by McKinsey found that high performers are 400% more productive than average employees, and in highly complex roles, the gap can reach 800%.[2] This productivity isn't just about individual output but also extends to how they *influence* the broader team and company performance. The research notes that these high performers drive better results, contribute to innovation, and elevate organizational culture.[3] Their influence often leads to higher profitability, improved customer satisfaction, and greater team cohesion.

Throughout this book, I will walk you through key aspects of building your foundation. Starting from setting the right tone at the top, to creating an attraction engine that will effortlessly draw high performers in instead of having to chase, to engaging with them on a deeper level by finding alignment and building rapport, and to the best practices that secure high performers at the sensitive decision-making stage.

The goal is to make recruiting the right people *easier* for your organization so you can stay focused on growing your business and serving your clients. This is more than an informational guide, this is a strategic tool for increasing performance and your bottom line.

There are several key themes in this book—themes that underpin my work as a strategic recruiter and have helped our firm become an industry leader.

One of the first principles I emphasize with my clients is that **having the wrong advocate, or the wrong "who" at any stage of the process, will significantly decrease your chances of hiring high performers.**

Having the wrong advocate will significantly decrease your chances of hiring high performers.

You can have a strong foundation—a great environment, a culture of excellence, and the right messaging—but if the *wrong* advocate is involved in the recruiting process, representing your company and articulating opportunities, that foundation will not maximize success in human capital. The wrong person can damage your company's reputation in the marketplace, devalue your brand, and undermine any alignment towards your vision.

Another theme we will discuss in depth is **quality versus quantity**. As a leader, your most precious asset is time. If you have a pile of resumes from candidates who do not align with your vision, then you and your team are going to end up wasting valuable time— reviewing, rejecting, and dealing with the pile—instead of turning your focus to more strategic endeavors. The goal is to relieve the administrative burden and work more efficiently. When you have a solid recruitment strategy in place, it is going to ease the burden and stress of hiring.

The goal is to attract and connect *only* with high-performing talent to begin with. Focus on quality, not quantity.

Your most precious asset is time.
Focus on quality versus quantity to achieve a higher
level of success within your recruitment efforts.

Most internal teams might be capable of doing this for lower-level hires, but when it comes to more strategic, high-impact roles, the complexity may become too much for them to understand and communicate effectively, and that inability can repel high performers who have a high interest in your company. Sometimes, the most efficient route is to collaborate with a strategic recruiting partner who has specialized expertise in the area you're hiring for.

The third recurring theme is the overlap between specific **sales strategies and recruitment practices.** In general, if you are great in sales, you know that you have to position every step, every communication point in the right manner. You cannot afford to be too aggressive because it will cost you the "sale" (the hire). You have to seek alignment by understanding what the "customer" (the candidate) desires. And you have to leverage quality over quantity.

In the war for top talent, *every* interaction matters. Your brand, your message, your culture has to be communicated in the best manner possible within every exchange when engaging with high-performing candidates. What your recruiting partner, your internal team, and your external messaging say about your company can all serve to increase your success if executed effectively or hinder your success if not aligned properly. Because every touchpoint, every interaction, has the power to *influence* the rockstar you want to hire, the rockstar who will ultimately transform your organization.

Every interaction matters. And **closing is happening within every interaction**, not just the offer stage. That is why the Build–Engage–Close Framework is so critical.

> *In the war for top talent, **every** interaction matters.*
> *Every touchpoint has the power to **influence***
> *the rockstar you want to hire.*

Lastly, this book will reveal the most common mistakes and provide useful, easy-to-implement strategies on how to avoid them. This includes everything from the wrong strategy, the wrong person, the wrong message, lack of rapport, lack of depth and detail, and having no sense of urgency in your interactions. We will talk about the all-important matter of **intentional alignment** versus misalignment and the need to articulate your company's vision clearly to attract the right talent.

If it sounds like a lot, well, it is.

This book is designed to take you through the most effective way to execute every stage of the recruitment process. That means digging into the details, giving you a fly on the wall view of interviews and vetting, sharing real stories from placing hundreds of candidates, and painting the picture of just how much a high performer can transform your organization—if you follow the Build–Engage–Close Framework.

A Transformative Recruitment Partner

I am passionate about helping high-performing companies and professionals find each other and grow together. I started my career in a client-facing role in public accounting during the cutthroat, performance-driven aftermath of the 2008 recession, which meant that if you were not contributing to growth, you were out. At a young stage in my career, I was fully immersed in financial statements and client relationships—and eventually grew to be a finance leader in the corporate world. I held roles in external auditing, financial reporting, internal controls, and finance transformation in professional services, mid-market, and Fortune 500 companies. And it was during this time I also achieved my CPA designation.

What carried through all my roles in my early career was my involvement in recruitment. Having worked inside multiple organizations, and being closely involved in the recruitment process, it became clear what worked, where the gaps were, and how certain actions—or inactions—led to breakdowns.

What struck me most was the way that **low performers demotivated high performers,** even in great organizations.

Having also been approached by recruiters firsthand, it was easy to spot the disconnects on that side of the process as well. The gaps were clear and so was the opportunity to do it better. As relationships deepened and opportunities to add the most value became clearer, the path forward began to take shape.

I found my passion lies in *alignment of talent and vision*. And ensuring growth-minded leaders that we partner with have access to rockstar talent that will make their lives easier.

The power of alignment drives me. **When values, goals, and skill sets align, hiring becomes transformational—not transactional.** The long-term success that follows benefits both the individual and the organization. So, I applied my skills and experience to develop best practices and deliver the right guidance to my clients. In 2017, I co-founded Selective Insight to help high-growth companies attract high-performing talent.

*When values, goals,
and skill sets align, hiring becomes
transformational—not transactional.*

My company has built a trusted network of high performers with decades in the industry, and from that vast network, we are now able to make introductions to rockstar talent within days. We have a 92% success rate from introduction to interview and 87% conversion rate from offer to acceptance (when the right strategies are used), and client retention rate nearing 90%, with long-term partnerships across professional services firms and high-growth companies backed by private equity, including L Catterton, Carlyle, CVC, and Littlejohn.

> *We have a 92% success rate from introduction to interview, 87% conversion rate from offer to acceptance, and client retention rate nearing 90%.*

The secret to our success is the Build–Engage–Close Framework. It is all about filling gaps and avoiding breakdowns. Even more importantly, it is about building trust, rapport, and alignment to help our clients hire top talent more efficiently. Because of our exceptional performance record, we have become a preferred partner for the majority of clients we have taken on. Now, I am direct and do challenge the way organizations think about and approach recruitment to serve their best interests. And that is one of the things that has attracted growth-minded leaders to utilize Selective Insight in their recruitment efforts.

In my recruitment practice, we consider it a disservice not to share best practices—because we are not interested in transactional relationships. We are deeply invested in helping our clients grow and succeed in alignment with their vision.

By reading this book, you will get all those insights and more. And ultimately, it's about more than just recruitment. Bringing in rockstars has the power to transform every aspect of your organization and your life. If you are the leader or aspiring executive of a growth-focused company who demands *excellence* and values top talent, strong relationships, and true alignment, then this book will take your recruitment strategy to the next level.

Regardless of industry, this framework will teach you how to win rockstar talent that will make a positive impact within your organization and align with your culture of excellence.

Finding the right hire is more than just an asset—it is a force multiplier for your organization.

One rockstar can transform the entire organization, significantly increase your bottom line, and provide measurable, maximum ROI for years to come. If you are a leader who refuses to settle for mediocrity and who understands low-performing employees are a liability, then this book is the right strategic guide to grow your company the rockstar way.

Turn the page. Let's start building.

CHAPTER 2

HOW THE LAW OF ATTRACTION WORKS IN HIRING

An invisible force. An irresistible energy. A compelling power that drives us toward someone or something great. The law of attraction tells us that *like attracts like*, and while this may seem like a simple, straightforward premise, the implications and uses of the principle are nearly infinite. If you can learn to harness the power of attraction with recruitment, it will revolutionize the way you hire and retain top talent. Because in the war for top talent, those who master attraction don't chase—they magnetize.

The **Build–Engage–Close**™ **Framework** shared in this book starts with making the law of attraction work for you and your business by using the three key stages of recruitment. We will begin by discussing the first element you need to win the talent war: **BUILD**. We'll cover the following:

- using the law of attraction to recruit top talent,
- winning clients using the law of attraction,
- how alignment without action does not lead to attraction,
- why your environment is the foundation of attraction,
- adopting a growth mindset to maximize attraction,

- what repels rockstars, and
- how attraction works in active vs. passive candidates.

What Is the Law of Attraction?

So, what is the law of attraction and how does it work? It may surprise you to learn that the law of attraction has roots dating as far back as the Greek philosophers, including Plato, who wrote that, "Likes tend towards likes."[4] This is the origin and the basis of the law of attraction. The law of attraction tells us that what we focus on directly determines what we attract. In other words, people with *aligned* values, goals, and beliefs are naturally drawn to each other, forming deeper and more meaningful connections.

Plato wrote that, "Likes tend towards likes."

In the modern era, the law of attraction has gained even greater popularity in fields like self-help and personal development, especially as our understanding of quantum physics, energy, and frequency levels expands. It has also been widely embraced by tremendously successful speakers, authors, and entrepreneurs like Tony Robbins, Oprah Winfrey, and even Henry Ford. We know that energy is the basis of everything in our tangible universe, yet do you know how to harness that energy to attract rockstars?

Using the Law of Attraction to Recruit Top Talent

The success of any company depends on the ability to attract and retain the best people. But despite the widely known importance of top talent, a recent study by McKinsey found that 69% of companies interviewed believed there was "a significant human capital or capability gap within their organizations."[5] Even more worrying, less than 8% of businesses expressed "high confidence in their end-to-end talent strategy (that is, recruiting, integrating, upskilling) to deliver the workforce needed to drive future growth." The study reveals a shocking disconnect between understanding the need for high performers and taking meaningful action to attract them.

Studies show a shocking disconnect between understanding the need for high performers and taking meaningful action to attract them.

So, why is the law of attraction so pivotal for companies who want to hire rockstars? If a company wants to hire a high performer who is going to positively impact their ROI, then the company must *build* an environment where values align across their organization. For example, if your company values excellence, and the rockstar loves to excel in everything they do, then the attraction builds organically and quickly. Oracle, Apple, Amazon, and Microsoft all recruit top talent who mirror their company's culture to build teams that will work hard, think creatively, and add long-term value.[6] That is because they know the importance of having high performers working for *you*—not the competition.

One critical item I want you to keep in mind, the goal is to have the attraction *build* throughout the entire hiring process, **starting from the first interaction**. Every detail matters to a high performer, and therefore your organization needs to pay attention to every detail to allow the law of attraction to work in your favor.

To attract rockstars consistently, you must be able to cultivate a compelling culture that aligns with the values and qualities top performers seek. Growth, challenge, continuous improvement, excellence—that is what they want to see in your environment. This alignment is critical. Without it, your environment will repel top talent as they'll quickly recognize a lack of growth, innovation, and opportunity for progression.

You as a leader play a crucial role in this process, as your leadership style and authenticity set the tone for the entire organization. Demonstrating that your company not only talks the talk but also walks the walk can turn potential candidates into enthusiastic team members, driven by a shared purpose and commitment to excellence. If you can accomplish this, then you will naturally attract high-caliber professionals who are, quite literally, "on the same wavelength," as you and your company.

I know this because it worked for me.

Winning My First Client Using the Law of Attraction

In 2017, I decided to leave my position as Director of Finance at a Fortune 500 media company. It was a big risk and a complete leap of faith. I would be starting over from zero. I questioned whether I was doing the right thing and if my plans would work out the way I envisioned them. I knew I wanted to transition into the executive recruitment space alongside my husband and business partner, who had twenty years of experience in the field. And so I went with my gut and told myself it *will* work out.

Once I made that choice, I put everything I had—all of my experience, technical knowledge, and energy—out into the world in order to attract new clients for our growing business. But I didn't want to attract just any clients, I wanted to attract and help the *right* clients.

STRATEGIC RECRUITER SCORECARD

*Key questions to determine if your recruiter
can deliver high performers.*

#	QUESTION	YES	NO
1	Prioritizes quality over quantity	☐	☐
2	Has deep expertise in your specific hiring niche	☐	☐
3	Understands what defines a high performer	☐	☐
4	Challenges hiring assumptions when necessary	☐	☐
5	Can provide references from at least two clients they've partnered with for 5+ years	☐	☐

Building Selective Insight wasn't going to come easy. But there was one thing I knew for certain: attracting the right client was going to be a direct result of **alignment.**

During this time, I took a lunch meeting with a friend and former colleague, Chris. We had worked together previously at a national advisory firm. The company (where Chris was still employed) had a great business model: they sought people with strong, intangible soft skills, people who aligned with the company's goals, and they knew exactly who they wanted to hire. This was something that had originally *attracted* me to the company, as I feel strongly that it is soft skills that drive the highest level of success in a leader. Technical skills alone limit the value a high performer can bring to the table. Mix strong intangibles with strong technical skills and voilà, you have increased your bottom line.

Chris and I chatted away over our salmon sushi rolls and steaming cups of green tea in the restaurant lobby of my former corporate office. The more I told him about my intended career transition to recruitment, and the more he talked about what his company valued, the more it revealed how similar we were and how much we had in common. We both shared a growth mindset, as did the company and its leadership. We were both personable, high performers, strong communicators, entrepreneurially spirited, analytically minded. And most importantly, we recognized the potential in one another. The *right alignment* was forming!

I also knew what could repel a rockstar leader (which we will discuss in depth later in the chapter), like Chris, and so I avoided making those mistakes. This meant that I was not going to sell myself to him, which can come across as inauthentic and desperate to true rockstar leaders.

Instead, I focused on developing strong rapport, which made for a seamless interaction and established trust between us. Our beliefs and values when it came to business were in complete alignment, alignment being that *je ne sais quoi* magic ingredient of professional success. So much so that we decided to work together again.

No, that did not mean I was going back to work for my old advisory firm. It meant that Chris wanted me to do recruitment for their firm! He introduced me to his talent acquisition team the next day.

Just like that, I landed my first client for our executive recruitment firm. They had such faith in me to serve their interests, despite the fact I had no track record as of yet in recruitment. That faith came, I believe, from the **law of attraction**. The talent acquisition team trusted Chris' recommendation, which was based on our "attraction," our strong alignment of values, our strong belief in a high performer's potential, and our high energy.

This advisory firm was my first client, and to this day, my company remains one of their top strategic recruiting partners. I credit this to the law of attraction, which works throughout a professional and personal relationship, from beginning to end. The attraction endures because we share the same alignment of values.

This experience proved to me that whatever you project out, you will receive in return. If you have that strong belief and an awareness of your energy, and you take the right action steps, the law of attraction *will* work in your favor.

Alignment Without Action Does Not Lead to Attraction

This leads me to the next point about attraction. A common misconception about the law of attraction is that belief alone is enough to "manifest" or materialize your desired outcomes, but belief without action will not work.

As we saw in the story above, I had a strong belief that my new endeavor would be successful, and I had attracted a great opportunity through my meeting with Chris. But I did not stop there. I knew I had to keep the momentum and the energy level high if I wanted to make it a success. Waiting around for something to happen would likely have meant missing the opportunity all together. So, my next step was strategic action.

After my meeting with the talent acquisition team at Chris' firm, I had to deliver. I had zero revenue to begin with. All I had was one client, and my partner—my husband and co-founder—had just secured one as well. Together, we set a deadline of three months to get our early growth company out of the nest, flying on its own. It took a relentless drive to make it happen.

We started having conversations with high-performing candidates in my network and making great leaders aware of our intention to branch out independently. As we built our brand and expanded our network, I leveraged my professional assets to attract more of the *right* candidates and clients. My CPA designation worked in our favor, helping us attract other high-performing CPAs, CFAs, and professionals pursuing highly respected certifications. That alignment of ambition and values built a foundation of trust. It was another case of like attracting like—the law of attraction demonstrating its power.

The same law of attraction applies to recruitment. Without the belief that you can consistently attract high performers, you won't— because a rockstar strongly believes in themselves and wants to work for a company that strongly believes in its mission, values, and ability to succeed. But belief alone isn't enough. You must also take intentional, decisive action to attract the caliber of talent you're seeking.

We see this all the time—people who expect good things to simply show up at their door without any effort on their part. I do not believe in that fairytale and neither should you. In the following sections, I'll share what strategic action you need to take to *maximize* the law of attraction in recruitment.

Your Environment Is the Foundation of Attraction

The first step in harnessing the power of attraction is creating the right environment and the right culture. This is the foundation, the first **building** block for creating attraction. If the foundation is unstable, the whole house comes crumbling down. You have to get environment and culture *right* before you can really think about attracting heavyweights. If you fail to do this, sooner or later the people you recruit will see through the cracks in the foundation and jump ship for a company that will fully utilize their potential and drive for excellence.

Top performers have a relentless desire for continuous growth and improvement. Those same qualities should be reflected in your environment. Create a culture focused on continuously improving, optimizing, and developing if you want to attract and retain top talent. If they see that the environment they are in is continually striving upward and improving, they see themselves as improving, too. *Like for like.* The company and its workforce should reflect one another in this way—that is the heart of alignment.

Create a culture focused on continuously improving, optimizing, and developing if you want to attract top talent.

Adopting a Growth Mindset to Maximize Attraction

According to a *Forbes Business Council* member, "Every successful company has a common theme: a growth mindset. Leaders with this mindset constantly upgrade their talent and playbook. They believe in being challenged, and they create high-performing teams that like to do better and be faster than yesterday."[7] If you do not have the talent component right, it does not matter how good your service, product, or technology might be, your company cannot succeed at the highest level. That is why you need to leverage the law of attraction.

"Every successful company has a growth mindset."

A rockstar is not going to be drawn to a low performer who doesn't have a growth mindset. For example, let's say you have an environment where the majority of professionals have no ambition, do the bare minimum, and leave at five o'clock every day instead of going the extra mile. If you introduce a high performer—who wants to excel, who wants to exceed expectations—what do you think will happen? Will the high performer be attracted to this culture? A mediocre environment is going to repel them. And I speak from experience.

When I started at the Fortune 500 media company, I was brought in by the CFO. He was amazing. He was high energy, he wanted to get things done, and he wanted to increase profits. We were two peas in a pod—the law of attraction. It was the CFO who pulled me into my role as Finance Director with the goal of transforming certain operational accounting and controllership functions. I had a mission, and the CFO shared my vision for it. I thought the rest of the company would be equally aligned with us.

However, when I got more involved with the wider organization, I realized everyone there was just kind of going through the motions. Few seemed interested in *excelling*. It was like being plunged into cold water. I had gone in with high energy and a drive to transform processes for the better, but being surrounded by team members who just could not be bothered was totally demotivating.

Every effort was made to get people on board—to spark some sign of life. But after six months, the energy it demanded became draining. Challenging work is normally fulfilling, and there's satisfaction in doing a job with excellence. But at this company, something shifted. Going to work no longer brought purpose, and it took a real toll on my mental wellbeing.

There's no sugarcoating it—I was depressed. Coming home each day, my husband would ask why I seemed so tired, so unlike myself. And he was right. It wasn't like me at all. It became clear the environment was no longer the right fit. The belief system in place rewarded the bare minimum, which clashed with my mindset built around continuous improvement, meaningful collaboration, and pushing past perceived limits. That experience played a major role in shaping the decision to build our business focused on high performers. No high performer should feel overlooked or underutilized. Yet too many top contributors remain stuck in roles or cultures that stifle their potential instead of unleashing it. I set out to align rockstar talent with rockstar companies—because I've seen firsthand the transformative impact a high-performing team can have. And I've also seen the cost of low performers who do just enough to get by.

What Repels Rockstars?

The opposite of the law of attraction is repulsion. **What repels high performers and how can you avoid that?** There are many times that I have heard a great candidate mention a horrible experience with a recruiter—including being overly aggressive and pushy to completely disengaged or indifferent. Even though they might not have been working with the recruiter directly in the new role, the experience was demoralizing enough to tarnish the company's reputation in their eyes. It killed their attraction to the hiring company.

The way your team interacts with a candidate, especially a high-performing candidate who puts their all into their career, is a make or break. Communicating with rockstars is an art. It should not be taken lightly. Finding a good balance between respecting their success and ensuring alignment with your organization is critical. Keep in mind these top three pitfalls to avoid when attracting a high performer:

1. Lacking growth opportunities.
2. Surrounding them with low performers.
3. Treating them like a resume instead of a whole person.

*Communicating with rockstars is an art.
Finding a good balance between
respecting their success and ensuring alignment
with your organization is critical.*

Are There Opportunities for Fast-tracked Advancement?

Nothing drives top talent away faster than the absence of growth opportunities. High performers are driven by excellence. Stagnation feels like failure to them. They do not want to be average. They do not want to just get by. They want to innovate. They want to beat benchmarks. They want to break new ground.

So, ask yourself, is your company providing opportunities for employees to progress consistently or be fast-tracked to the next level? Do your incentive packages reward additional efforts? What type of opportunities do you provide your rockstars to pivot within your organization? What kind of upskilling programs and continued learning do you offer? For example, Google implemented the Googler-to-Googler network, which gives employees a means to learn from each other, collaborate, and improve on one another's ideas.[8]

Low Performers Repel High Performers

The next element that can negatively impact your ability to attract a rockstar is having them interact with a low performer. **If one of the first interactions a high-performing candidate has with your company is with a low performer, it will repel them immediately.**

This is true whether the interaction is with an internal recruiter, team member, or leader in your organization, or even if it is an external recruiter who is advocating for your company. If you put an average person across the table from a high performer, it is going to flash like a warning sign to the high performer. There is no sugar coating it. That's a fact. The only momentum you are creating in that interaction will be the rockstar running as fast as they can in the opposite direction.

Rockstars Are More Than Their Resumes

The third thing to avoid is treating a high performer like just another resume during the recruitment process. If they get the impression that you are simply conducting a box-checking exercise, drilling them with preset questions, or that you are only paying attention to their technical skills, it is going to be a turn off. Why? Because you are failing to build rapport.

A high performer wants to show you who they are and the potential they have. They cannot do that if all you are focused on is bullet points on a PDF. That is going to read as average and uncreative. If there is no strategic thinking, dynamic exchange, or genuine rapport involved in every interaction, starting with the first conversation, then the candidate will see that as a reflection of the wider culture.

The bottom line is this: if you're looking to attract exceptional talent, and your own top talent is not involved in the process, you will not achieve your recruitment goals. And let's not forget leveraging the right strategic recruiting partners. The best way to avoid pitfalls two and three is to assess which specific person you want to engage in each step of the process. **When someone is advocating for your company, you want that person to be the best representative possible.** The law of attraction tells us that we receive what we put forth. If you have a low performer representing your team, you are going to repel a high performer. But if you have a rockstar at the front of all interactions, then you are going to attract other rockstars— *consistently*.

So, as you prepare to select your representative, first ask, what is their track record? What have they accomplished? Have they displayed excellence in their career? If they have not, the law of attraction is *not* going to work in your favor. That is key. Secondly, you should assess their communication skills. They should be able to articulate at a deep level and pivot the conversation to learn about what the candidate brings to the table.

Interactions throughout the recruitment process should never be a "one size fits all." You also want to avoid an interaction sounding like a sales pitch. The exchange should be organic. Conversations should flow naturally.

Imagine, for instance, that you are recruiting for a mission-critical position. If the employee conducting screening calls is a first-year hire—because they are the one with time for what is viewed as "low-value tasks"—what signal does that send to the rockstar candidate? If the recruiter they interview with is a low performer who has no track record of being promoted within their role, what does that say about how you are valuing the high-performing candidate's time, abilities, and knowledge? You want to show candidates from the beginning that you see their worth and recognize their potential—and will value it accordingly. Ultimately, you want to seek and ensure alignment between candidates and the people *doing* the recruiting.

How Attraction Works in Active vs. Passive Candidates

One final point about the law of attraction is to distinguish between *passive* versus *active* candidates. A passive candidate is someone who is not actively searching for a new job, or they are casually looking elsewhere but are not ready to make the move. A passive candidate is thinking about whether there might be better opportunities for them with another company, and they would likely commit if they felt strongly that they found a position they were more aligned with.

In contrast, an active candidate is exactly that, someone who is actively looking for a new job, actively pursuing opportunities, actively engaging their network or a recruitment firm, and actively taking interviews. They have already made the decision to leave their current role.

It is important to know whether you are dealing with an active or passive candidate. The law of attraction is important for both, but it is even more critical if you want to attract passive candidates. Passive candidates are open to discussions about new opportunities, but they tend to be much more measured and discerning. Any misstep in the recruitment process, like the ones outlined above, will repel them instantaneously.

That means you need to turn the volume up to eleven when it comes to utilizing the power of attraction with passive candidates. Keep the energy high and make sure you have the *right* person in place to recruit them. A passive candidate with in-demand skills will only want to leave their current role if they feel a deep connection to your company, alignment with your vision, and can believe in the opportunities for growth. Be sure to pay attention to every single detail within the recruitment process if you want to nail it. Again, **attraction comes from alignment**.

You might ask yourself, why extend additional efforts for a passive candidate when an active candidate is more eager? Recruiting passive candidates is like landing a marlin instead of a guppy. It may take more energy to reel them in, but they are worth every ounce of effort for the value and energy they will bring to your business.

The Law of Attraction in Action

Thus far, we have covered what the law of attraction is, why it matters if you want to attract the best people, how to harness its power and avoid pitfalls, and the difference between recruiting active versus passive candidates. Now let's put it all together. What does the law of attraction look like when correctly applied to recruit exceptional talent? Let me give you an example.

We partnered with a high-growth company to find a rockstar manager for their finance team as they were rapidly expanding their presence across the U.S.

I found a candidate who was a rockstar. At the time he was a senior level associate, not yet a manager in his current role, but he was exceptionally high performing. The only reason he had not become a manager was he was inherently limited in his current environment. There was no room to grow, and he felt he was not being challenged enough for his skill level and interest. Hence why he was looking for a more promising opportunity. It was important to him to find alignment in his next role, given his unsatisfactory experience in his current company.

As he went through the interview process with our client, they did everything right to generate excitement and engagement. They gave in-depth details about the company's growth plans. They outlined which specific opportunities he would have for promotion, including a fast-track for advancement in exchange for additional efforts. The CFO had a growth mindset and recognized the high potential of the candidate, and thus, was able to share a one- and three-year projected plan for where the candidate could be within the company if he were fast-tracked. The candidate was deeply motivated by that.

It was a great fit, especially because there was uncapped growth potential. They aimed to flip the company within five years, making it critical to have the right people in place to maximize value during that window. Once the candidate was hired, he wasted no time going above and beyond, taking on additional responsibilities and making everyone's lives easier by his proactiveness. All because the CFO believed in his potential based on his traits as a high performer combined with his foundational technical skill set. And that is how the law of attraction is meant to work—and how it can work for you.

Now that we understand how the law of attraction works to effectively engage rockstar talent and the importance of aligning recruitment strategies with the law of attraction, how can you build your own **Rockstar Attraction Engine**? In the following chapter, we will take a deep dive into how to build a culture of high performance, starting with your recruiting strategy, marketing strategy, and messaging strategy.

RITA'S INSIGHTS

- *Like attracts like*, which means if you want to hire high performers, your company must embody high performance.
- You can use the law of attraction to win top talent through alignment of vision, values, and growth mindsets. Clearly communicate your company culture, growth opportunities, and future vision to keep high-performing candidates engaged and excited.
- Keep the energy and momentum high! Always put your best foot forward within each step of the recruitment process. That means leveraging strategic recruiting partners and your own high performers at the helm of the recruitment process.
- Remember, the first interaction with a rockstar candidate is critical. Don't repel a high performer by engaging a low performer in the process.
- Determine whether a candidate is passive or active, and tailor your recruitment strategy accordingly.

CHAPTER 3

BUILD AN ATTRACTION ENGINE IN THREE EASY STEPS

Attraction is the driving force behind winning over people who will grow your company. And that is why it is very critical to build what I call a ***Rockstar Attraction Engine***.

The three key components are:

1. The Advocate
2. The Brand
3. The Message

These three elements are like the spark, fuel, and oxygen needed to start a fire. If you want to light a fire within your recruitment strategy—one that will keep on burning and generating energy within your company—then this is what you need. It is what will keep your momentum high in attracting great talent and keep the vehicle of recruitment moving forward.

Attraction Engine

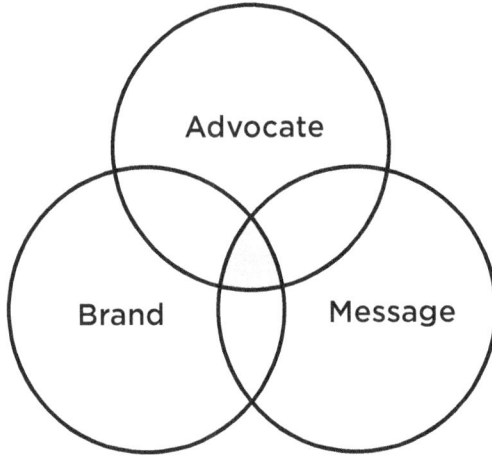

```
                Advocate


        Brand          Message
```

What are the specific elements of the advocate, brand, and message? How do you produce the best possible version of each so that you can attract the best possible people? How can you optimize every single step to yield the outcome you want—that is, securing a rockstar?

Regardless of industry or size, every organization has room to improve its recruiting process. Great leaders have vision. They can see the business they want to create—one filled with high-performing people who deliver incredible ROI, a vibrant culture that inspires everyone to give their best, and a clear, exciting message about the purpose and impact of what they do. But even the most preeminent leaders among us do not always know how to achieve those goals. It may be because they are too busy with the actual running of the company, or because recruitment is outside their field of expertise.

For many companies, recruitment requires deliberate, time-intensive efforts—especially when organic attraction is lacking.

However, if you can harness the power of attraction, then the people you want will come to you. They will be drawn to your business rather than you having to chase them. In this chapter, we will break down the three key elements of building a Rockstar Attraction Engine, so that recruiting rockstars becomes organic and built into the DNA of your business. If you get these three components right, then attraction evolves into a natural extension of the business itself.

Your Advocate: The "Who" Matters Most

Remember, attraction equals influence. That influence occurs at every stage of the recruiting process. And every stage contains certain communication steps. **A candidate's first interaction with your company—whether it is with an external recruiter or internal team member—is the start of your influence.** That is why the "advocate" part of the equation is most important.

The right voices championing your company turn it into a magnet for exceptional talent. When the right people advocate for your business, transformational growth is inevitable. What matters most is *who* you choose to put across the table from rockstar candidates if you want to build an attraction engine the right way.

When the right people advocate for your business, transformational growth is inevitable.

The *first* interaction between the advocate and the rockstar candidate sets the tone for the whole relationship.

Imagine you are going out on a first date with someone. You know the basics about each other, but you have never met in person before. If you go to dinner and that person spends the whole time speaking about themselves, never asking you more than a superficial question before taking back control of the conversation, will you feel a connection to that person? If they show signs of aggression towards the wait staff or worse, you, would you go on a second date? Or imagine you do manage to hit it off well, but the date tells you that they are only looking for something short-term and nothing serious. That is the equivalent of telling a rockstar candidate that there is no room for advancement in their role. And it is likely to end the conversation, or as I like to say, *the first interaction ends up being the last interaction.*

> *Don't let the first interaction with a rockstar candidate be the last interaction.*

A high performer will be turned off by any of the scenarios above. Forget about moving forward. Forget about this being a successful recruitment strategy. People who know their own value will look elsewhere, to people and companies who acknowledge their hard work and recognize their talent. They have options—and they will take them.

It may come as a surprise to learn that a lot of hiring companies get this wrong. *Who* you choose to represent your company may seem like an insignificant detail. You may think, "Well, it's just an introductory conversation. How important can it be? I don't want to waste my time or my top performers' time with this." Or even worse, "Let's use the cheapest external recruiter to attract top talent for us." But remember, *closing* is always happening with each and every interaction.

That initial interaction is tremendously important. **You only get one chance at a great first impression.** It is your opportunity to build rapport and demonstrate that you care about the rockstar candidate as a whole person. I'll talk more about building rapport later in the book.

You Only Get One First Impression

There are simple steps to take to make sure you avoid a "bad first date" interaction. Bear in mind that the first interaction is sometimes informal. It may be a casual conversation, formal interview, or even a coffee chat. Regardless of what form the interaction takes, the person (your advocate) engaged with your recruitment efforts is the face of your organization for all intents and purposes, whether that is an internal or external party. Make sure your advocate is a skilled communicator. They should be able to ask insightful, thought-provoking questions that go beyond a simple technical checklist, delving into what truly drives rockstar candidates and aligns with your culture and vision. "The talent you attract is directly proportional to the quality of the questions you ask," as music industry giant Lou Adler said. Technical skills are important, but they should never be the starting point.

Your advocate must also be thoroughly familiar with the candidate's LinkedIn profile, resume, and any other important information relevant to the candidate. Preparing for any interaction, including an interview, is the responsibility of both sides if you want to demonstrate values like respect, diligence, and alignment.

*"The talent you attract is directly proportional
to the quality of the questions you ask."*

– Lou Adler

For a candidate who has put their heart and soul into their career, who wants to increase the success of your business, there is nothing more offensive than walking into an interview and just being drilled with questions—especially questions that are only surface level. There needs to be more depth in the questions asked and of course, rapport needs to be built first. It is an insult to them if there is no depth in the conversation, and they will see that lack of effort as a reflection of the company culture as a whole.

It is also a failure to not acknowledge or mention their achievements. It is a missed opportunity to build rapport. Recognizing their accomplishments not only shows respect for their expertise but also reinforces their value, making them more engaged and excited about your company.

Just like you want a good date to walk away thinking, "Wow, they showed genuine interest in me. I can't wait to see them again," you want a candidate to think, "This person really took the time to do their homework and learn about my background. They really care about getting *me* in the role—not just anyone."

When interacting with a high-performer, the advocate should tailor their approach based on what will appeal to a high performer. Let's say your company offers the ability to be fast-tracked to the next level without hitting a specific tenure mark, and you also offer a very competitive equity award or bonus structure. If you continue to emphasize the financial piece during the interview phase, it is not necessarily going to attract a high performer. It might even repel them because it suggests you don't understand what *really* motivates them.

Rockstars are more interested in progress and promotion within their career. Of course, they want to be competitively compensated, but if the growth opportunity is not there, then neither is the attraction.

Where companies often go wrong is in thinking that everyone wants to work for their company—regardless of the hiring process and what candidates learn about the company through that process. That may be true for low-performing or average employees, but rockstars are not like that. Not only do they want to work for a company that matches their commitment to excellence, but they will also have selective options to choose from at their discretion.

This is not to say you need to go overboard with flattery. You do not need to shower them with compliments. You should, however, acknowledge their achievements as a starting point. For example, "I've seen your success in creating financial models to increase visibility within your company. Tell me a little bit more about that."

Even better, where is there common ground between your advocate (your internal team member or external strategic recruiter) and the candidate? Is the candidate part of a specific community, which university did they attend, which specific certifications do they hold—and is there someone in your organization from that same community or university or that has the same certification? Use the commonality to your advantage to help create a connection. Asking these questions and putting the right advocate in front of the candidate can make all the difference.

The bottom line is this: whoever is recruiting on your behalf must understand that there is a high level of sensitivity around the *first interaction*. You can lose the best candidate—someone who would be a great ROI—because of an unattractive first interaction. **The goal is to have people on the frontline who know how to increase the momentum during each step of the recruitment process.** It is also why having a strategic recruiting partner is often the best approach. We will delve into further detail on this subject in the next chapter, but it is important to note here.

You can lose the best candidate—someone who would be a great ROI—because of an unappealing first interaction.

Build a Market-Leading Brand

The next element you need to light the fire of the Rockstar Attraction Engine is *brand*. When we talk about brand, we are talking about the culture and environment you create within the company. It is the image you want your brand to be known for, which can seem illusory at times. How do you build a brand? It starts with the trust and rapport you build within your team, the strong sense that you *care* about them as whole.

This is a big selling point for high performers, and it is what we mean when we talk about culture, which is not the same thing as perks (and many companies confuse the two). Don't get me wrong—perks are great. Candidates and employees appreciate benefits like wellness centers, ping-pong tables, and break rooms with a top-notch coffee machine. But perks are not the same as culture. They're just a starting point.

A brand starts with the trust and rapport you build within your team. The strong sense that you care about them as a whole.

Remember that ultimately you are dealing with a person, not a product. What counts in building an attractive brand is the intangible items that benefit a person as a whole. Be explicit when it comes to recognition. Show that you care about their progression.

Great companies offer fast-track lanes and have interactions with candidates on a personal level. The goal is to create genuine connections that go beyond professional experience—because the most sought-after talent chooses companies where they feel valued and recognized, not just employed.

Meaning and Motivation

One of the clients that I have had since the inception of our company, a professional services firm, is truly exceptional at ensuring that there are no barriers to success for people who want to work for it. They are an industry veteran that has withstood the test of time because they know how to attract and retain high performers.

At their organization, there is no arbitrary tenure mark that gets in the way of reaching the next level. Progression is dependent on an employee's efforts. And they offer extracurricular activities that form a deeper relationship with the talent that they have.

This is another gear in the attraction engine: appealing to people on a *personal* level. Rockstars are seeking alignment with a brand that matches their energy, values, and commitment to growth.

For example, this company regularly hosts speaking engagements, coaching sessions, and other events led by subject matter experts to motivate, inspire, and transform employees. The speakers they invite are not necessarily from the same industry, and they do not necessarily have anything to do with employees' day-to-day jobs. Instead, these events are investments in the long-term relationship with their employees to consistently help them grow both personally and professionally.

I recall one motivational speaker, Simon Sinek, who asked the audience whether, in the era of smart phones and social media, if we put our phones down when we are with our kids, with our families, with our friends? For a room full of highly motivated professionals, it was a revealing moment. It struck a real chord with people. The temperature in the room shifted. It was clear that everyone was reflecting seriously on this specific question. That one little question seemed to transform lives in that moment. People walked away with a renewed commitment to be more intentional when spending time with loved ones by putting their phones down and cherishing their time together.

Moments and opportunities like this are important for two reasons. One, employees want to feel seen by their employers, and that is even more true for rockstars. Offering opportunities that enable them to feel like a complete person goes a long way towards igniting and maintaining that sense of attraction to your organization. It creates a sense of loyalty, belonging, and deep connection. It shows you understand and want to meet their needs and desires, well beyond a simple paycheck.

Offering opportunities that enable rockstars to feel like a complete person goes a long way towards igniting and maintaining that sense of attraction to your organization.

Secondly, creating an environment that helps people *better* their personal life and enrich their relationships has a positive impact on their work. Researchers at Oxford University and the MIT Sloan School of Management found that happy workers are measurably more productive.[9] If your personal life is smoother and happier, there is a direct positive correlation to how you perform at work and how you function in your career.

In contrast, "Unhappiness at work costs the world $8.8 trillion in lost productivity," or roughly 9% of global GDP.[10] Those are losses you should strive to avoid.

The best investment you can make is in creating an environment that supports:

- Personal and professional fulfillment
- Productivity
- Sense of purpose

The evidence shows that, "The most important part of [talent recruitment] is to never stop thinking about your employees' potential and talent. No other factor is likely to make such a big difference when it comes to building a high-performing team."[11] Invest in your culture, and it will pay dividends for years to come.

Happy workers are measurably more productive. "Unhappiness at work costs the world $8.8 trillion in lost productivity," or roughly 9% of global GDP.

Growth-Mindset Leadership Goals

Leadership is another major facet of building a brand that will attract rockstars. **The tone at the top directly impacts whether your company becomes a magnet for rockstars or a revolving door of mediocrity.** There are two primary archetypes when it comes to leadership:

1. Growth-mindset leader
2. Fixed-mindset leader

A **growth-mindset** leader is someone who is focused on continuous improvement, and high performers will naturally align with this type of leadership. The concept of growth-mindset leadership was first formulated by prominent psychologist, Carol Dweck, who spent decades researching and observing leadership styles, culminating in her 2006 bestselling book, *Mindset: The New Psychology of Success* and her popular TED Talk, *The Power of Believing You Can Improve*. Since then, her findings have since been replicated in hundreds of other studies.[12]

According to one recent study, "A growth mindset can elevate your performance, determine how much money you make and even contribute to revenue growth for your company."[13] That same study found that 89% of senior leaders agree that future business success will depend on leaders who embody a growth mindset and an overwhelming majority report higher productivity, performance, and employee engagement as a result.[14]

"A growth mindset can elevate your performance, determine how much money you make and even contribute to revenue growth for your company."

Growth mindset leadership extends to growth on a personal level, and may include offering formal programs for personal development, coaching, and leadership training. (It is also a big part of the "Engage" component of the Build–Engage–Close™ Framework.) Does your leadership encourage improvement and push people beyond perceived limitations? Do you offer employees the opportunity to pivot and leverage their skill set in different areas of the business, rather than just an increase in responsibilities? These are all signs of growth mindset leadership.

However, if a leader has a fixed mindset, there will be strong misalignment with rockstar talent because a fixed mindset by definition creates a self-imposed ceiling on potential, limiting individuals' and companies' ability to reach their full capability.[15] A high performer will not be attracted to an opportunity at a company led by fixed-mindset leadership. Why would they commit themselves to an environment that puts limits on their achievements? Growth is part of the attraction. It is also mutually beneficial because having strong internal leadership translates to better optimization, collaboration, and communication.

Having strong internal leadership translates to better optimization, collaboration, and communication.

Be sure to highlight elements of your brand that appeal to high performers throughout the recruitment process to add to the spark of attraction. The top three areas to emphasize are:

1. Growth-minded leadership,
2. Opportunities for continuous personal and professional development, and
3. A culture that explicitly acknowledges and rewards high performance.

This is another way of "closing" throughout the recruitment process.

Master Your Messaging

The final element of the rockstar attraction engine is the *message*. This includes:

- Accurate articulation of vision and expectations,
- Published content,
- Success stories from employees,
- Testimonials from both tenured employees and customers, and
- All written and verbal communication that occurs within the recruitment process.

To begin, you must have clearly defined your mission, values, and vision. What sets your company and culture apart? As you reflect on this question, remember that the old saying holds true: **you cannot be everything to everyone**. If there is confusion in the marketplace about your brand or your values, it will impact the traction you have with rockstar talent and partners.

Think about what is most important to you and to the talent you want to attract. *Simplify* your messaging: don't emphasize everything all at once. What is going to resonate the most with a high performer? Where are you most likely to find alignment?

Then, once you have a powerful message based on your mission and values, **build assets to explicitly promote your brand**. You can do this by leveraging employees' success stories, bearing in mind that storytelling is all about depth. The message must move beyond the now commonplace and rather generic message, "I love working for this company."

Think strategically about which case studies and success stories are going to work for you in the long term. Creating a quality asset takes time, and you want it to pay dividends for years to come. As my mentor always says, "Build it once, and let it work for you for years, not just for the next quarter or 12 months."

Build an asset once, and let it work for you for years, not just for the next quarter or 12 months.

Seek out and use stories about how your workplace has transformed an employee's personal and professional life. How has the environment made them a better person? Interview team members who have experienced successful progression within the company from a lower role up to the VP level and beyond. These are the types of narrative that attract high performers.

Use these assets to share your message across channels. Employ them as part of the recruitment process to build momentum with rockstar professionals. Publish and share these assets strategically, especially on LinkedIn and through direct communication with candidates. Video is a powerful tool because it captures the energy, passion, and culture of the people behind your brand.

Why are testimonials and success stories so pivotal in amplifying the message behind your brand? Think about the recruiting process as being similar to making a big purchase online. Before clicking "add to cart," a smart consumer will do their research and look up reviews. If a product has no reviews, then you are not going to have any confidence purchasing it. Likewise with a one or two-star review, which tells you the product is not worth the money. However, when you see a five-star review, it instills a sense of conviction and certainty about the quality of the product and the customer service that comes with it. You are going to buy it without hesitation.

The same is true for top talent—they are certainly going to do their due diligence on any company that is wooing them. If they see an employee success story that resonates with their own vision and drive, what do you think is going to happen? They are going to get pulled in. The attraction generated by the testimonial then builds confidence in their decision-making process regarding your company.

Attraction Engine Failure

To illustrate the importance of the *Rockstar Attraction Engine* trifecta— advocate, brand, and message—let me share a story. It came to the attention of my friend, an equity partner of a large global organization, that his team was struggling to hire high-performing talent. They were constantly getting bombarded with low performers and individuals just going through the motions. Think of this like the red engine warning light popping up on the dashboard of a Rockstar Attraction Engine.

He and I had an in-depth conversation about the challenges he was facing within talent acquisition. When he raised concerns about his department's ability to attract the right people, I pivoted the conversation in that direction. It was an opening to develop our business relationship on the recruitment side, since that is my area of expertise.

I began by asking him about what his team was looking for as they sought to expand. And I kept asking questions to uncover what he thought was impeding their recruitment strategy.

"Do you know what the messaging is around your brand and the actual opportunity you are offering? What are the recruiters saying to candidates about your firm?" I asked.

"I'm not sure actually. I never thought to ask," he replied. Though I did not say this to him directly, it is a huge mistake—and a very common one—to *assume* that your company's representatives are doing things the way you want them done without direction. Frankly, it is a process that appears so basic that most people in leadership positions do not think to ask.

"Okay. What about conversations around growth? I know you have ambitious growth plans. You seem to be a great leader—it is why you were brought in as a Partner. Do you know if your team and external recruiters are emphasizing your transformative growth plans when they are speaking with great candidates?"

Again, he was not sure. So, I gave him some suggestions to take back to his team. We spoke the next day after he had time to dig into what was happening. And let me tell you, he was not happy with what he discovered.

"You were right," he began. "What our team has been saying to candidates is completely misaligned with the leadership's vision for the company. They have botched the message entirely. No wonder we can't attract and hire the right people."

It was a shock to the system. His "advocates" were not talking about the company's new vision at all. The organization was conducting a massive strategic overhaul that included lots of new innovation and automation of many of the more mundane administrative tasks (which is music to the ears for any high-performer). So, while the company was undergoing this revolutionary transformation that would set them apart from their competition, candidates were completely unaware, despite the fact that this would be an incredible selling point for any rockstar.

The problem was clear: the *wrong* people were delivering the *wrong* message about the brand. It was a huge attraction engine failure.

The good news was, now that he was aware of the issues, they could be addressed and corrected. He took immediate action to refocus the message on the strategic, transformative aspects of the open roles, rather than the generic job responsibilities that you would find at any average company.

Don't allow the wrong people to deliver the
wrong message about your brand.

Is Your Rockstar Attraction Engine Firing on All Cylinders?

The best companies sometimes do not always think through the recruitment process in such a methodical, studied way. But when they do, and they pay very close attention to every detail of their own Rockstar Attraction Engine, they instantly increase the likelihood that they are going to secure a rockstar.

The three elements of the Rockstar Attraction Engine work in unison throughout recruitment, whether it is the first email exchange, a 45-minute Zoom call, or an hours long lunch meeting. Your advocate, your brand, and your message must be firing on all cylinders if you want to keep the momentum high with a rockstar.

Because *who* you have representing your company is the first and most important part of the Rockstar Attraction Engine equation, it can be hugely beneficial to engage a strategic recruitment partner who has the specific skill set to find and land exceptional talent. In the following chapter, we'll explore when to engage a strategic recruiter and answer common questions about what to look for and what to avoid.

RITA'S INSIGHTS

- Your advocate, brand, and message are the three magic ingredients for lighting the fire that will propel your Rockstar Attraction Engine.
- The advocates involved in recruitment for your company must be excellent communicators. They must be capable of developing meaningful rapport, pivoting to what resonates, and forming deep connections with top talent.
- Do your homework! Know what appeals to high performers, emphasize growth, and highlight opportunities for progression in your messaging and throughout your marketing assets.
- "Closing" is happening incrementally in *every* interaction. That means that if you pay close attention to every detail within your advocate, brand, and message, you significantly increase the likelihood of securing a high performer.

PART II

ENGAGE

CHAPTER 4

HOW AND WHEN TO ENGAGE A STRATEGIC RECRUITER

Strategic recruitment is a kind of alchemy. It appears simple on the surface, but it takes particular skills and deep knowledge to assess the precise professional ingredients needed to produce hiring gold. In this chapter, we will delve into:

- Who is the best strategic recruiting partner for you,
- Why your company's own team members may need continuous guidance to stay in alignment,
- What happens when you engage the wrong recruiter and the damage that can cause to your company, and
- Hiring the right recruiter to help with your hiring goals.

At the end of this chapter, I will share an interactive set of questions that you can use to assess potential strategic recruitment partners.

"You're Not Like Every Other Recruiter…"

Let me share a story with you that highlights the theme of this chapter: that having the *right* strategic recruiter can make a world of difference to your company—in brand and reputation, financial savings and ROI, efficiency and performance, and more.

We partnered with a high-growth company looking to hire a strategic VP of Finance. Pretty straightforward, right? Now, an average recruiter would have just taken that request as the starting point to ask for a job description, salary requirements, and benefits package, so that they could begin to shop around to a pool of generic candidates.

Not me. My first instinct was to ask questions and make sure they were hiring for the *right* role for their particular situation.

As the conversation unfolded, a deeper question emerged: "Why is it you're looking for a VP level hire? What is your vision for how this person is going to collaborate with other team members? Are you looking for someone who is going to be in all of the details, or are you looking for someone with more of a big-picture perspective and a hands-off role in your finance function?"

The CFO paused. "You know, we really need someone who is willing to do the kind of detail work you mentioned. Leadership is happy with the strategic vision they've set. We need someone to do the work implementing that vision."

That set off a little alarm bell in my head. "That's good to know. Typically, when I see someone at a VP level, while they have the experience and knowledge to understand the details, they generally want to be less involved in the day-to-day. They want to be overseeing people. They want to be making decisions and setting strategy. They've progressed past the details stage of their career. Someone already at the VP level is going to see that as a step down," I said. "Can I make a suggestion?"

"Yes. What do you think?"

"I would suggest bringing in someone at a managerial level who's high performing. A high performer is going to have a short learning curve, and they are going to dive into those details with tons of motivation if you give them the opportunity and incentive to then progress to that VP position."

"I never thought of it that way," he said. "That's a great idea. Let's try it."

I introduced them to a high-performing managerial level candidate, who they decided to hire. And it was a huge success story. The new hire was eager to progress to the next level quicker, was willing to do—with excellence—whatever it took, and was loyal because he was given this amazing opportunity to be fast-tracked in his career.

And the company won on two fronts: they secured a high-performing candidate who did everything they needed and more, and they saved financially because they were able to hire for a position with a lower salary expense. Had they hired someone already at the VP level for the role, that person would have been demotivated by the lack of alignment between their responsibilities and their professional level. And the company would have lost time and money because of it. Instead, they were able to accomplish much more with less because we recognized a gap in their hiring process that they had missed.

In the following sections, we will discuss a few of the key insights that differentiate my company's approach to recruitment from everyone else. We focus on deep connection and alignment, draw from wide-ranging experience in both the corporate and client service worlds, and are not afraid to challenge assumptions if it is going to make your life easier and better!

Go Deep to Keep

It may sound counterintuitive, but recruitment is not just about filling a role. A good strategic recruiter does more than accumulate a pile of resumes. They know how to look at the technical skill set of a candidate, but even more importantly, they know how to identify and assess a candidate's alignment with the company they are recruiting for.

The more trust there is between a recruiter and candidate, the greater the candidate's attraction to the company.

If you want to retain someone long-term in your organization, then there has to be a deeper connection between the candidate and the company. And research proves this. A 2014 study in a marketing journal showed that the more trust there is between a recruiter and candidate, the greater the candidate's attraction to the company.[16] This might mean alignment on values, vision, or culture—whatever it is, there has to be something more that maintains and even grows that connection to your organization. This goes back to the law of attraction. And that is the element we want to focus on.

Look Under the Hood

As demonstrated in the story at the beginning of the chapter, part of the process involves considering your organization's actual needs. It happens more often than you might think that what a client *wants* is not the same as what a client *needs*. When a client approaches me looking to fill a particular role, my first response is not to immediately start pulling candidates and resumes. Instead, I like to gather more information to guide the process, pausing and asking, *Is this really the role they need to hire for?*

Gaining clarity starts with inviting the company to provide a snapshot of how things are functioning today. For example, if the goal is to hire a controller, I ask questions about the current accounting and finance team. This reveals more about the company's needs and helps clarify what kind of candidate would be the right fit. In other words, time is taken to look under the hood and understand how the business function truly operates.

This is a very important step—and one that most miss—because there might be a gap in how a company is thinking about its team structure and dynamic. Take the example of a company wanting to hire a controller. This is a role that has the ability to work cross functionally across multiple service lines, business units, and teams. I have found on more than one occasion, after speaking in depth with the CEO, CFO, and other leaders, that the better option was to transform their accounting operations and processes by leveraging automation and innovation in their financial operations, making them more efficient and returning a greater ROI than simply hiring an additional employee.

A one-size-fits-all recruiter, which does all the hiring for the whole company, is not likely to have the specialized knowledge required to identify gaps like this. The differentiator is having the ability to assess the details, not just surface level, to conclude what a company actually needs in order to increase ROI and to make your life easier.

Having been in public accounting and the corporate world, I have seen under a lot of hoods, so to speak. I started in client service examining accounting and finance controls and operations. It was my job to find the gaps and identify areas where things could go wrong. I've seen companies struggle, time after time, making the same mistakes. And when I moved to the corporate world, I was finding inefficiencies and conducting and executing process improvements for mid-market up to Fortune 500 companies.

Successful companies operate differently from struggling ones. The best execute with the precision and speed of a Formula 1 pit crew, making the exact adjustments needed to stay ahead on the final lap. At that level, industry best practices are instinctive, and every move is calculated for advantage. When something's off, it's like a slow tire change—the loss of momentum is immediate, and everyone watching knows it. When it comes to your recruiting, would you rather have a chop shop cowboy or a Formula 1 pro looking under the hood of your company?

Would you rather have a chop shop cowboy or a Formula 1 pro looking under the hood of your company?

Challenge Assumptions

The most successful companies in the world, like Apple and Google, have leadership that welcomes challenge. It leads to continuous improvement and growth. Business research supports this, showing that a culture of positive, constructive challenge can help to mitigate risks and improve decision making.[17]

Other recruiters, who are *not* focused on excellence or attracting high performers, are more likely to be "yes men." They will tell you what you want to hear, even if it is not the best thing for the company. As long as they are making money, they do not want to rock the boat.

Strategic recruiters care deeply about their work, about their clients, and about the rockstar candidates they introduce. And they have the unique expertise and industry perspective to know where improvement, changes, or pivots can be made to improve efficiency and ROI. That means they are going to say it how it is. They are the best friend that gives you the hard truth you need to hear that no one else has the guts to say.

Is Your Team Up to the Task?
Lessons from Phil Jackson

Phil Jackson, the "Zen Master" of basketball, won 11 NBA championships as a head coach not just because of talent but because he **mastered the art of getting the best out of every player.**

His formula was simple yet profound. Find the right people, develop their strengths, and create an environment where the team's mission outranks personal glory. Jackson had an uncanny eye for potential, not just skill, but mindset and chemistry. He knew the difference between a good player and a great one often came down to how well they *fit* the system.

Once he had the right mix, he invested in their mental toughness, emotional intelligence, and adaptability. His leadership blended strategic precision with deep human understanding. He motivated Michael Jordan differently than Scottie Pippen, and he handled Shaquille O'Neal differently than Kobe Bryant—*tailoring* his approach without losing sight of the team's larger goals.

Jackson brought mindfulness, trust, and accountability into daily routines, something rarely seen in professional sports at the time. This built a culture of shared responsibility, where **every player understood their role and believed in the mission**.

The takeaway is clear: building a championship team starts with finding the right people, developing their full potential, and creating a culture that thrives under pressure.

Phil Jackson built his teams by seeing beyond the stat sheet. Finding the right mix of talent, mindset, and chemistry, then developing each player's full potential.

Unfortunately, in many companies, the hiring process looks nothing like that.

Most have limited scope and influence. They operate under what I call the "checklist trap" (which I'll explain in the following pages) and often struggle to connect deeply with candidates due to perceived company bias.

In this section, we'll break each of these elements down.

Limited Scope

There is a common misconception that if someone is in a role, that they automatically know what they are doing. The reality is attracting and engaging high performers isn't something you learn in school or by working at a single company. Mastering the art of communicating with top talent and building meaningful rapport comes from diverse real-world experience.

How do you identify the right person to attract and engage top talent? High performers want to connect with those that are like them. Like attracts like. The person in the recruitment seat should have relevant experience, deep knowledge, and a proven performance record.

High performers want to connect with those that are like them. Like attracts like.

The Checklist Trap

In the last chapter, we talked about the importance of a growth mindset, rather than a fixed mindset, when it comes to leadership that attracts rockstars. The same principle applies to hiring and the mindset of your talent acquisition team.

Very often there is a fixed mindset in the process of recruiting. Hiring is seen as a process of checking off boxes or searching for keywords in a resume and only interviewing those candidates. This is the absolute wrong approach if you want to hire high-performing professionals.

This approach is guaranteed to overlook potentially great candidates. If your team cannot assess people beyond a basic technical skill set, then they also do not have the requisite knowledge to identify a high performer, someone with potential and drive to progress. They are going to miss markers of strong leadership qualities, and they may even miss out on accurately assessing a candidate's track record of success—metrics that make all the difference to your ROI. All of that is thrown out the window.

The bottom line is this: if your team is just looking at a list of keywords from a job description, then they are stuck in a fixed mindset, and as a result, they are missing out entirely on this beautiful grey area of talent that can transform your whole team.

Connection Is Everything

It cannot be emphasized enough how much connection matters to high performers. In a wide-ranging study on employer image and branding, researchers found that **a recruiter's "warmth and competence" positively and measurably improved candidates' image of the company.**[18] The influence was so impactful that they found even candidates who previously lacked confidence in the company could have that negative image reversed by the *right* recruiter.

Whoever is doing the recruiting for your company must be able to create real connections and develop deep rapport if you want to attract rockstar talent. The stronger the connection, the higher likelihood that the recruiter will be able to influence the person and secure them for your company.

Additionally, candidates are more likely to trust someone outside the organization to provide an unbiased view of the company and its culture. Candidates, especially intelligent, observant candidates like high performers, will perceive the bias existing employees have, and even positive things they say about the company will be taken with a grain of salt because, *"They have to say that. Of course you are going to say great things about this company, you are part of it."*

> *Candidates are more likely to trust someone outside the organization to provide an unbiased view of the company and its culture.*

In contrast, a strategic recruiter situated outside the company automatically has a greater degree of credibility because they are perceived as having greater transparency and less bias. My job focuses on finding people and companies that align with one another. I have to find people who are the right fit and who will remain with the organization long-term if I want to uphold our company's reputation and commitment to excellence. We take on the responsibility of creating deep connections and meaningful rapport with high performers. In my work, trust and credibility are everything.

Wrong Recruiter, Big Disaster

So, now we know that your internal team may sometimes need external help with attracting top talent, but it can be difficult to distinguish a good recruiter from a bad one. How do you go about finding the *right* strategic recruiter? And what happens if you hire the *wrong* one?

It is a critical decision, and the right choice may not be obvious from the start, but the damage done by the wrong recruiter can last for many years. I have seen firsthand what happens in the fallout. Having heard horror stories from clients and candidates about other recruiters who bully, lie, misrepresent companies, use harmful pressure tactics, waste companies' precious time and resources, and do lasting brand and reputational damage to the very organizations they are meant to help.

And let's be honest, we have all heard these stories. There are recruiters out there that will keep pushing the goalpost, lying to candidates and companies just to make a quick buck. There are dishonest, unethical recruiters out there. As a leader, you will know this, too. Just how bad can the wrong recruiter be? I want to share a quick story with you to illustrate just how important this is.

"You're just a low-level staffing firm."

When I first started working with one of my clients, a management consulting firm, I quickly started to realize there was a huge disconnect between the image and messaging I was receiving from leadership within the company and the feedback I was hearing from professionals who had been in contact with other recruiters *about* this company.

The consulting firm was in the process of a strategic expansion. They were interested in attracting high performers to build out their vision, but they were struggling to do so, despite working with multiple external recruiters. The recruiters were bringing in huge volumes of candidates and resumes, but only one out of every 100 or so applications was the right fit to be hired.

Now, I am very selective in both the candidates and companies I work with. And this company was amazing. It offered attractive growth opportunities and implemented cutting-edge strategies. They should have had no roadblocks in recruiting rockstars. So, what was the problem?

Come to find out, the issue was with the other external recruiters. They put forth average recruiters and butchered the messaging about the company. The low-level recruiters had no idea how to engage with high performers, and they gave off the impression that the whole company was low level, fixed, and stagnant. It destroyed any confidence or trust that candidates had in the company.

The recruiters said nothing about the growth opportunities or transformation happening at the company. In other words, having the wrong advocates for their company disrupted their whole brand image and what they were trying to build. There was a total lack of alignment on values between the external recruiters and what this organization was about.

As soon as I discovered this through conversations with people in my network, I brought it to the attention of the client.

"Do you know what they're saying about your company?" I asked. "They are telling candidates that you're just a staffing firm, a low-level staffing firm. You're not strategic."

To say the client was shocked is an understatement. Staffing companies are very different compared to top-tier management consulting firms like this one. Staffing companies are not known to be strategic. They are lukewarm bodies at a desk. But this company was focused on solving complex problems for the office of the CFO. They had worked hard to build a rockstar culture, and here they were being portrayed and marketed as a low-performing staffing firm.

It completely derailed the company's brand. After I raised the alarm, the company took action. They decided to cut a lot of the external recruiters that had been dragging their brand through the mud. It did not happen overnight, but they were able to slowly build their image back. We helped them recruit the talent they were actually looking for, rockstars who would work hard and take advantage of all the opportunities for growth.

It was a real shift for the company. One executive put it this way, "So, is this what it's like to work with a good recruiter?" And it does make a world of a difference. A good strategic recruiter will be aligned with your company's vision. They will act like a megaphone for your company's focus on continuous improvement, great leadership, and the quality service that you offer. And a good recruiter strategically collaborates with your company to positively impact your success and growth.

Reasons to Hire the Right Recruiter

The main reason many companies hesitate when it comes to hiring an external recruiter is cost. Every great leader is constantly thinking about their ROI, financials, and expenses. The right strategic recruiter is expensive, but they are expensive for a reason. It is because they are delivering results consistently, not just for one role or two, not for just one year or two years. They deliver rockstar talent consistently year after year for decades.

A low-cost recruiter might save you money in the short term, but they will cost you far more in the long term. In the words of inventor and innovator Red Adair, "If you think it's expensive to hire a professional, wait until you hire an amateur."

It goes back to the law of attraction. A less expensive, low-quality recruiter is going to attract a less expensive, low-quality person. Like attracts like. I have seen it time and time again. And I have never seen a recruiter with an inexpensive fee that produced huge results. You get what you pay for.

Maybe you're thinking, so what? If there is a red flag in the hiring stage or issues early on because the low-performing candidate isn't up to par, then you have to fire them and start over. What's the big deal?

According to the U.S. Department of Labor, a bad hire can cost your company 30% of the employee's first-year earnings. Some HR agencies estimate the cost to be higher, ranging from $240,000 to $850,000 per employee.

The big deal is that there is a heavy cost to mistakes in hiring. According to the U.S. Department of Labor, a bad hire can cost your company 30% of the employee's first-year earnings.[19] Some HR agencies estimate the cost to be higher, ranging from $240,000 to $850,000 per employee.[20] And the higher up in the organization the bad hire is, the higher the cost to your company. Do you want to eat those kinds of costs again and again just to save on recruiter fees in the short term?

Qualities of the Right Recruiter

There are three key qualities that the right recruiter will bring to your hiring process that cannot be imitated by anyone else:

1. Trust
2. Relief
3. Influence

Let's look at each quality and how it can take your recruiting strategy to the next level.

The right recruiter has access to talent others can't reach as they have built long-term trust and relationships. In recruiting, trust is currency. And those who've earned it in the marketplace consistently deliver better results.

In recruiting, trust is currency. And those who've earned it in the marketplace consistently deliver better results.

Who has a greater likelihood of attracting top talent? Someone limited to internal resources, or someone with the reach, influence, and access beyond the organization? Of course, it is the latter: a strategic recruiter.

When you leverage the right strategic recruiting partner, it gives you a better pulse on the marketplace. They can help your company stand out from the competition because high-performing candidates can trust what they hear from the recruiter as an independent, transparent advisor.

In the right environment, candidates often share sensitive questions they may hesitate to ask directly to the hiring company. For instance, it's not uncommon for candidates to ask questions like, "I saw negative feedback in a review online. Are you able to tell me if this is accurate?" or, "I am starting a family in the next couple of years. Are they supportive of that?" This is an opportunity to advocate for the client and provide specific examples that emphasize alignment (or misalignment). It is also a chance to build confidence and alleviate any concerns they may have.

A strategic recruiter can openly talk to rockstars about their goals, personally and professionally, with greater candor. They are not limited to just talking about the numbers or falling into the "checklist trap." We can go beyond the surface level details. Candidates, understandably, are not comfortable sharing too much personal information with their potential employer, but these are the kinds of considerations that can make or break a successful hire.

Next, let's talk about how a strategic recruiter positively impacts mental wellbeing. **When your recruiter understands your vision, leadership style, and only brings in talent aligned with both, your mental bandwidth improves.** You're no longer wasting energy on misaligned hires or constant backfilling. That's a major advantage of working with a true strategic recruiting partner.

A strategic recruiter is there to save you time, energy, and money. Many clients have shared how much frustration we've eliminated by taking recruitment off their plate. It allows them to delegate the mental load of attracting and engaging high performers—freeing up focus for more strategic leadership. Just as important, it spares them from the costly missteps and poor-quality hires that often come from relying on overstretched HR teams or low-level recruiters.

The biggest advantage of hiring the right recruiter is *influence*. As we know, *like attracts like*. High performers are drawn to other high performers. That's why leveraging the right high-performing recruiter can influence them far more than an average one. That is a huge benefit to securing top talent.

Influence is one of those intangibles that can be hard to define, but in this context, it means a combination of skills, including:

- Building rapport,
- Communicating with excellence,
- Applying technical expertise, and
- Knowing how to close.

An excellent strategic partner is one that can execute all of these skills at the highest level. That's what I've learned.

An influential recruiter is someone who can identify gaps in the company's hiring strategy, who intuitively finds alignment between companies and candidates, and who has an instinct for potential.

Let's also keep in mind that human interaction is never a one-size-fits-all approach. It's an art form—and it must be treated as such. Your strategic recruiter is not just filling roles. They're reading nuance, adapting in real time, and shaping impressions that directly influence who says yes to your offer.

Human interaction is never
a one-size-fits-all approach.
It's an art form and it must be treated as such.

You may be able to make the case that an internal team knows the company culture better than an external recruiter. But do they understand and know how to interact with high performers, and are they able to attract the best talent? Just because they know the culture does not mean they can communicate it well and can accurately and energetically represent everything your brand has to offer.

Do's and Don'ts of Hiring a Recruitment Specialist

There is a lot that goes into assessing a recruitment specialist. All of those elements have been distilled into five simple questions that will help you determine whether someone has the expertise to recruit rockstars for your organization. Be thoughtful and honest as you work through these questions to make your assessment.

STRATEGIC RECRUITER SCORECARD

Key questions to determine if your recruiter can deliver high performers.

#	QUESTION	YES	NO
1	Prioritizes quality over quantity	☐	☐
2	Has deep expertise in your specific hiring niche	☐	☐
3	Understands what defines a high performer	☐	☐
4	Challenges hiring assumptions when necessary	☐	☐
5	Can provide references from at least two clients they've partnered with for 5+ years	☐	☐

RITA'S INSIGHTS

- The law of attraction applies to the relationship between the recruiter and candidate. The more trust that is built between them, the more attraction the candidate will feel towards your company.
- The *wrong* recruiter can cost you—not just financially—but also in long-term damage to your brand and reputation. The *right* recruiter will save you time, energy, *and* money.
- A good strategic recruiter is able to identify gaps in your hiring process that others miss, engages rockstar candidates on a deeper, more meaningful level, and accurately assesses alignment.

Since you're reading this, it's clear you're committed to hiring the best. If you'd like to discuss how I can help you attract and retain top talent, reach me directly at *rbaroody@selectiveinsight.com* or visit *www.SelectiveInsight.com*.

CHAPTER 5

THREE SALES TACTICS THAT WIN TOP TALENT

Where the first phase of the Build–Engage–Close™ Framework is all about building the foundations of your organization and recruitment strategy using the law of attraction—your company, leaders, culture, environment, and strategic partners—the "Engage" part of the equation involves the interactions you have with candidates and recruiting partners.

This isn't sales in the traditional sense, but I've observed that recruitment is remarkably similar to sales in many respects. And it makes sense. When you're luring top talent and trying to align rockstars with rockstar-worthy companies, you're basically "selling" a human resource. In this chapter, we will discuss the *three sales tactics* that will transform your approach to recruiting:

1. *Avoid being too pushy or aggressive.*
2. *Always seek alignment.*
3. *Leverage quality over quantity.*

Be the Lure, Not the Fish

Imagine you're on a first date, and within five minutes, the person across from you says, "We should get married. You'd be perfect for me." You'd run, right? Even if it is the most attractive person you have ever seen and they share all the values that matter most to you, your instinct would kick in. It is just too much, too soon.

Recruiting works the same way. If a recruiter comes on too strong—pushing an opportunity without understanding the candidate's aspirations—it backfires. High performers are not desperate. They are thoughtful and selective, and just like in dating, they want to feel pursued for the right reasons, not just because they fit a generic checklist of skills.

The first sales tactic to leverage for recruiting high performers is to avoid being too pushy or aggressive. A lure draws the attention of the fish, and the fish will chase the thing it wants (an opportunity with your company!). Don't be the fish—chasing after the bait, even after it has been pulled out of the water.

> *As CEO Gary Vaynerchuk noted,*
> *going in hard for the sale right away*
> *will not get you anywhere.*

Most high performers tend to be analytical, forward-thinking, and strategic planners by nature. They are not going to get swept up in the moment or make impulsive, emotionally-driven decisions. So appearing overeager or pursuing them too aggressively is not going to come across as persistent, enthusiastic, and determined—it is going to seem annoying, demanding, and desperate. The more you chase, the faster they run. Or, as CEO and entrepreneur Gary Vaynerchuk noted in his *New York Times* bestseller, *Jab, Jab, Jab, Right Hook,* going in hard for the sale right away will not get you anywhere.

A soft approach fosters trust and builds momentum gradually. The research supports this approach. **Critical contact theory** shows that because candidates' knowledge of potential job roles is limited, they are more heavily influenced by the recruiter than by the actual attributes of the job, and the recruiters' behavior (e.g., being friendly and competent vs. aggressive and incompetent) provides important signals about the attractiveness of a given position.[21]

Critical contact theory shows that candidates are more heavily influenced by the recruiter than by the actual attributes of the job.

Persistent or Pushy?

Persistence is valuable in both sales and recruitment, but there is a clear and significant difference between being persistent and being pushy. So, what are the signs of a pushy sales tactic? At what stage do touchpoints become pain points? Volume and content are big indicators. If a recruiter is sending multiple messages to candidates, especially messages with generic content, it is going to send them running for the hills. High performers want to be pursued, yes, but they do not want to be hounded.

Again, there is a surprising amount of overlap between recruitment and dating (probably because so much of recruitment is about relationship building). If someone is constantly blowing up your phone—even if you really like them—you are likely going to see that as a red flag. And it is even worse if those messages are generic because then not only is it irritating, it also gives the impression that you are one of many. That they are not really interested in *you,* they are just playing a numbers game.

Another sign of pushiness is when a recruiter pressures a candidate to accept a role despite signs of *misalignment.* Trying to push a rockstar towards a role that does not meet their drive for excellence and need for growth is like trying to fit a square peg in a round hole. It is never going to work. Some things cannot be forced. Even if they accept the role, somewhere down the line, that misalignment will eventually lead to disagreements or dissatisfaction.

These examples may sound extreme, but it does happen. And that is not how you want your brand to be represented. I have seen it happen with great brands that do not even know that this is occurring in the background. It can be hugely damaging to an organization's reputation, not to mention the untold losses by missing out on high ROI rockstar hires.

Don't Give Up on the Grey Area

One area of critical distinction between sales and recruitment lies in what I call the *grey area.* Salespeople can often be quick to put potential clients in a box: yes or no. They only pursue prospects they know they will close right away. And many recruiters operate that way, too, especially those who are constantly chasing fees. Their viewpoint can become very binary, to the detriment of finding the best candidates for your company.

That is because many high performers, as we have said, are deliberators and thinkers. They are not going to jump at the first opportunity presented to them. They are more selective. But they are also going to be open to hearing about opportunities that align with their vision and goals, even if it is something they had not considered before. In other words, **rockstars do not fit into neat little boxes.** They might not be an immediate "yes" or "no."

In my experience, high performers can fall into the grey area. Give them time to determine whether there is real alignment between them, the role, and your company. Take a softer approach, do not expect a yes or no from the start, and use that time to build the relationship. Follow up in a few business days when they have had the time and space to make the best decision on whether or not to move forward. Don't give up on the grey area. Trust me, it will work in your favor!

High performers can fall into the grey area.
Give them time to determine
whether there is real alignment between
them, the role, and your company.

The Golden Rule for Rockstars

A significant number of recruiters in the industry are opportunistic and transactional. Their strategy is to get someone in the role, regardless of fit or performance, because they are banking on the fee they earn when their candidate gets hired. It may sound blunt, but if you have been in the industry long enough, you will have also seen this for yourself. And if a recruiter's primary focus is on their fee, then they are certainly not focused in the right place, and they are going to fumble or even repel high performers.

A money-focused mindset tends to make recruiters pursue candidates more aggressively. Though it took me a while to fully understand, I experienced it first as a job seeker. On more than one occasion, I had recruiters push roles on me that I was not interested in. When they questioned why and insisted that such and such was a great company, I had to remind them that neither aligned with my goals nor how I wanted to grow in my career. Many of them disrespected my value and failed to acknowledge the effort and dedication it took to achieve a professional designation.

Eventually, I had to block certain recruiters who kept pushing. Those kinds of experiences stuck with me because they left such a sour taste in my mouth. And on the flip side, I valued recruiters who were not pushy, who asked insightful questions, and wanted to build a relationship.

When the transition into recruitment began, those experiences shaped how our team would go to market: by focusing solely on building trusting relationships with candidates (no pushy tactics). So, when one of our early clients commented that the approach felt "different," it raised the question—was something being done wrong? Was the client being let down? It even sparked internal doubt about whether the team should take a more aggressive approach, like the tactics observed from other recruiters.

But I always remembered how I felt when approached by aggressive recruiters, and that drove the decision to focus more heavily on relationships (versus transactional interactions). As time went on, we gained confidence that our approach was actually the right approach. We saw great results consistently, which came as a direct result of how we treated candidates. It was the Golden Rule but for rockstars—*treat rockstars how rockstars want to be treated*. That is the proven approach that resonates most with high performers. This leads us to the next sales secret: **alignment**.

The Golden Rule applies to recruiting high performers: treat rockstars how they want to be treated.

The Single Most Important Factor: Alignment

Selling is all about relationships, and the same is true for recruitment. This is why *alignment* is so important. Great salespeople understand the value of building long-term relationships with clients as loyalty is necessary for longevity. Top salespeople learn to think like their clients. They learn their needs, desires, and goals so that they can anticipate and fulfill them. You don't succeed in sales by convincing someone to buy something they're fundamentally not interested in. You succeed by finding buyers who have a problem that your product or service can solve.

Alignment—mutual goals, shared values, and a deep understanding—is key to achieving all of that.

Use this **Alignment Checklist** to evaluate each candidate against the following criteria:

1. **Role Competence**
   ☐ Possesses the foundational technical skills, knowledge, and experience to excel in the role.

2. **Growth Mindset**
   ☐ Demonstrates the ability and motivation to expand skills and take on greater responsibility.

3. **High-Performance Track Record**
   ☐ Experience consists of high achievement with a commitment to excellence.

4. **Cultural Fit**
   ☐ Values and priorities align with the organization's mission and long-term vision.

5. **Problem-Solving Ability**
   ☐ Approaches challenges with creativity, resourcefulness, and sound judgment.

6. **Adaptability**
   ☐ Adjusts effectively to new environments, challenges, and is versatile.

7. **Reputation**
   ☐ Ethical, builds mutual respect, and treats stakeholders as partners.

8. **Collaboration**

☐ Works well with others, can influence, and elevates team performance.

It is always better to know if there is misalignment early on in the process because once you know a person is not a good fit, you can move on—saving you time, energy, and money. You would not want to sell something to someone that they don't need and don't want. Likewise, a good strategic recruiter will not keep pushing an outcome when they know there is misalignment. It is not about forcing a fit.

> *It is always better to know if there is misalignment early on in the process, because once you know, you can move on.*

Where does misalignment usually come from? I have heard from many organizations that usually when someone is not a good fit, more often than not it is because of their intangibles, their soft skills. In the following sections, I will give you some key insights on how to assess these notoriously difficult to pin down candidate characteristics.

The **subjective factors theory** suggests that candidates seek a fit with the organization or with the type of job being filled. The perceived fit results from the degree to which their personal characteristics align with the characteristics of the prospective job and organization.[22] An in-depth meta-analysis on attracting high-performing candidates found that fit, also known as alignment, is the single most important factor in successful recruitment and attraction outcomes, stating it had "strong effects" and played a "substantial role" compared to every other factor.[23]

Alignment is the single most important factor in successful recruitment and attraction outcomes.

Not every rockstar is aligned with every culture. A recruiter's primary purpose is to discover where that alignment is. To do that, you need to paint the picture, listen more than you speak, and ask deep questions that get to the heart of alignment.

Paint the Picture

As mentioned earlier, recruitment and human interaction is an art. A recruiter needs to be able to create meaningful rapport by asking the right questions and pivoting the conversation to uncover alignment or misalignment. It is a process of building trust to achieve better outcomes—for everyone.

There's a simple principle to keep in mind—**paint the picture**.

Paint the picture of alignment by asking the right questions.

Paint the picture of alignment by asking the right questions. Deeply learn about the rockstar candidate in front of you, and then grab that paintbrush and emphasize the areas that are in alignment with the candidate's goals, beliefs, and aspirations.

It is also important to be fully transparent throughout the process, as this fosters trust and open communication. Once you paint the picture in the right manner, the candidate will be instantly sold—no pressure, no aggressive tactics required.

Listen More Than You Speak

We have talked about rapport building often in this book, and that is because it is so essential to connecting with high performers. A great sales tactic you can apply to recruitment is to listen more than you speak. In sales, the idea is that the buyer knows their needs better than anyone. Instead of spending time and energy convincing someone to buy a product, it is better to listen to what their pain points are so you can speak directly to their needs and highlight specific solutions you can offer.

In recruitment, it is similar. **Make it about the candidate first**. As you get to know rockstar candidates on a deeper level, listening is one way to learn about their needs and wants, as well as what they can offer your company. By the end of the first conversation, they will be far more open to your influence—because they'll feel you genuinely understand their goals, needs, and what they're seeking in a role and company.

Just like the example from the start of the chapter, if you have ever been on a date with someone who would not stop talking about themselves, you know how excruciating that can be. No one wants to date someone with a massive ego, and no one is going to respond to a recruiter like that either.

The Deeper the Questions, the Better

You are never going to find that spark of connection with a high performer if you only ask about technical skills and the same tired questions interviewers have been asking since 1975. You won't truly understand who this person is, whether they align with your company's culture, or if they have the qualities that will make them an effective leader in your organization if you only focus on asking technical questions.

The deeper the questions you can ask, the better. Now, I am not suggesting you start off with hard hitters or deeply personal questions, but you have to be able to *pivot* the conversation when the time is right. In the next chapter, we will get into the specifics of rapport building, vetting, and interviewing, including sample questions to inspire candidates, but for now, we will just say that this is an important sales strategy you can apply to recruitment. As billionaire founder of Virgin, Richard Branson, said, "Hiring the right people takes time, the right questions, and a healthy dose of curiosity."

> *"Hiring the right people takes time, the right questions, and a healthy dose of curiosity."*
>
> – Richard Branson

Let's keep in mind: high performers are not like the average job seeker. They are passionate and have worked hard to get to where they are, and they will respond better throughout the recruitment process if you begin with a positive note. Give them praise. Acknowledge their success. Recognize their achievements.

This is key to being successful in "selling" a rockstar. It works in sales because the more deeply you understand a client—what is important to them, what they value, what they need—the better you can tailor your solution. The same is true in recruitment, only in this case, the more you know about a candidate, the more you are able to assess whether there is alignment.

A Tale of Two Pictures

I want to share a story of how alignment worked profoundly in a client's favor when recruiting a standout, high-performing candidate. Throughout the recruitment process, we asked deep questions about what she valued, what was important to her, and who she was as a person, beyond the technical scope of her work. We built strong rapport and trust.

From this process, I learned that she highly valued work-life balance and building relationships with like-minded people. Because she was a rockstar, she received multiple offers, including an offer from one of our clients. The other offer came from a company that I did not have visibility into.

She was struggling to make a decision and was leaning towards the offer with the other organization. Because we had built strong rapport and trust, she came to me for advice on the offers. The role with this other entity was for financial due diligence in their mergers and acquisitions department—a position and environment I was very familiar with. It was an extremely technical role and a very demanding one at that. So, I painted the picture for her.

"Listen, this is a great opportunity, but you are going to be working nonstop. That is fine for some people, but I know you value work-life balance. You will need to work crazy hours and probably most weekends. Does that align with what you want?"

She laughed. "You know, it doesn't. And what about the other offer? What is that environment like?"

That was a very different picture. She would need to put in the effort, which she was happy to do, especially since our client offered lots of opportunities for growth and progression. But her weekends would be free to spend with her family and pursuing her hobbies and interests. It would be a better balance, which is why she set out on her job search in the first place.

I painted both pictures, and it was clear where she aligned. Finding that alignment meant she was able to make a better decision, and the company gained a valuable high performer who was more likely to stay with the company because of their shared vision and goals. Ultimately, there was no need to push.

The alignment that you identify between a candidate and your company should be leveraged throughout each step of the recruiting process to yield the best outcome.

The alignment that you identify between a candidate and your company should be leveraged throughout each step of the recruiting process to yield the best outcome. We will talk more about this in the next chapter, but just remember this is a key insight for engaging rockstar candidates.

Quality Over Quantity Is a Competitive Advantage

Most recruiters favor a quantity over quality approach. They think of recruitment as simply a numbers game, and the more candidates they have in the pipeline, the more fees they earn, regardless of the long-term outcomes for the company or the candidates. So, they cast a very wide net. They might even use certain tools to send *thousands* of emails and messages—because it is easy to just push a button, even easier now with AI.

It is even worse with companies that engage multiple recruiters. Now, imagine a rockstar candidate getting five messages about the same exact opportunity from five different recruiters. How are they going to perceive the hiring company? It is going to appear that your employment brand is diluted and the desperation is all the way up. And it is going to repel high performers from engaging with your company.

This strategy, if you can even call it that, is to provide a high volume of resumes to a hiring company, with no real thought or effort to the conversion rate. Both the recruiter and the company in this scenario are focused on quantity. The goal is to see how many resumes they can acquire rather than how many candidates they can convert to employees. But really, what does a 1 percent conversion rate achieve? Who is that helping? Who wants to sift through 100 resumes? In reality, this strategy wastes time, energy, and staff resources. There is no way to meaningfully assess that many candidates.

On top of seeing the quantity approach as a waste of time and energy, I have also seen how damaging it can be to an organization's brand. If you have worked hard to create a culture of excellence, then the last thing you want to do is dilute your brand through mass marketing and hiring the wrong people. It will ruin your reputation in the marketplace, tank your ROI, and take years to rebuild your brand back to what it was before.

The last thing you want to do is dilute your brand with mass marketing and hiring the wrong people.

If you have been reading along this far, you know that our approach is the opposite. *Quality over quantity* is the bedrock of selective, aligned recruitment. If you want rockstars on your team, quality wins the debate every time. When it comes to resumes, the best strategy is smaller pile, higher conversion.

When it comes to resumes, the best strategy is smaller pile, higher conversion.

Salespeople refer to this as "throwing darts" versus "casting nets." When you cast a net, you're trying to scoop up as many fish as possible, just an undifferentiated mass of seafood (not to mention all the other undesired matter your nets pick up).

But when you throw darts, you're targeting your efforts at prime candidates who are more likely to "convert." As any salesperson will tell you, a small number of highly qualified leads yields better results than a pile of names on an unvetted list.

This approach has meant that I often go against the grain of the industry standard. Often at the start of a relationship, a client might push me for more options. It takes time for them to adjust to the "new norm" of the quality over quantity approach, meaning that if I present them with three high performers, and every single one is amazing and aligned, only then do they realize that they do not need 100 resumes to choose from. They just need three rockstars. Client Testimonial

Shifting from the quantity to quality approach is a lot like getting out of a bad relationship, and it's true—a lot of companies have been stuck in bad relationships with low performing, quantity-based recruiters for years. They are accustomed to the constant cycle of hiring and firing low performers because they have been told that is the norm, and they are just supposed to deal with it.

It is not until someone shows you a different approach, lessens the frustration and the time taken, the drain on your energy— not until someone makes your life easier and puts your brand on a pedestal that you realize there is another way, *a better way*. Would you rather have high volume and low conversion or low volume and high conversion?

*Would you rather have high volume and low
conversion or low volume and high conversion?*

Like any strategic recruiter or any good salesperson, we want a successful outcome. But we also know that the priority should be fit versus volume. Recruitment is really a process of refinement. There is no way we are going to present a client with an unfinished product, which is how I view a pile of 100 resumes. It's the reason our exceptional network has been built over the years—to drive referrals and bring high performers through the door.

In the next chapter, you'll see exactly how you can achieve this—by mastering the vetting process and building meaningful connections with candidates.

RITA'S INSIGHTS

- Critical contact theory tells us that candidates are more heavily influenced by the recruiter and the recruiter's behavior than by the actual attributes of the job. So, if a recruiter is pushy and aggressive, that is going to send the wrong signals about the job and your company.
- Don't push for a "yes" or "no" right away because high performers often fall into the *grey area* and require a softer approach.
- Alignment is *the* most important factor in successful recruitment outcomes. You can find out whether a candidate is aligned by asking deep questions, listening to their goals and values, and painting the picture.
- Quality over quantity will give you a better ROI, provide lasting longevity in your hires, and elevate your brand in the marketplace.

CHAPTER 6

FIND OUT WHO THIS ROCKSTAR IS THROUGH STRATEGIC VETTING

Every stage in the recruitment process is important yet the vetting process is one of the biggest stumbling blocks for most companies. As we now know, studies show that candidates are more influenced by the person recruiting them than by the actual attributes of the job, and candidates look to the recruiter's behavior as a key indicator of the attractiveness of the role they are applying for. That means it is extremely critical that every part of the vetting process, where the recruiter and candidate are starting to interact on a deeper level, is done right.

So, how do you find out who this candidate really is?

In this chapter, I will share the secrets of vetting and building rapport that will help you recruit rockstars. We will look at **how to keep momentum high**, the **optimal cadence for communication**, using a **strategic recruiter to foster trust and openness**, and **best practices for building rapport**.

We will also discuss how to spot red flags and identify misalignment early in the process, which are just as critical to finding out who this person is and whether they are the right fit, and we will explain how a successful recruiter vets candidates.

Maintain Momentum

The first secret to keeping rockstars engaged is to keep the momentum *high*. These are high performers. They are dedicated to excellence and always thinking about the next step or the next five steps—and they do not want their energy to go to waste. As the hiring company, you want to show them that you are on the same level and share that high energy.

If we go back to our comparison of recruitment and dating, we can see how momentum impacts the perception of the relationship being built. If you go on a great date with someone, but then you do not hear from them for several days, what would you assume? You will think they are not interested, right? The same principle applies to recruiting—silence sends the wrong message. The candidate wants to feel valued and respected. Maintaining the momentum and staying connected is essential to demonstrating that value and respect.

The secret to keeping rockstar candidates engaged is to keep the momentum high!

Why is momentum so important? Well, a rockstar has up to three or more companies reaching out to them *on a daily basis*. That means you should also assume they are in the final stages of recruitment with other companies: either they have an offer on the table already, or they are about to receive one. If you want to be successful in recruiting a sought-after high performer, then you need to translate this assumption into a high level of urgency throughout the process. Always think about how you can keep the process moving forward and keep this great candidate moving along with you.

How can we increase momentum with a rockstar candidate? Be explicit about your interest. You do not want a high performer walking away from an interaction feeling unsure about how the conversation went. Don't be afraid to be direct! It can be as simple as telling them, "I enjoyed learning more about you. I would love to continue this process and introduce you to other team members." This is music to their ears because it means they know where they stand with your company. I hear this feedback from candidates all the time. They want to have a firm sense of their progress and ability to move forward.

Now, this doesn't mean that you have to go overboard! When you've gone on a few dates with someone and the connection is building, it raises the stakes when one person takes initiative and says, "Hey, I really like you, let's see where this is going." Don't do the recruiting equivalent of impulsively, prematurely blurting out "I love you!" on the first date! Just be direct and honest without being overly enthusiastic.

Timing Is Everything

You might be saying all the right things to candidates, but that will not matter if the timing is not right. Where momentum drives the overall pace of the recruitment process, timing is about the cadence of reaching specific benchmarks in your communication with candidates. And I see a lot of companies get this wrong, in part because they think the ball is in their court during the recruiting process, but when they create communication lags, ultimately, they find they are left playing that game on their own.

Your company might be extraordinary, but that does not mean your team members have prioritized responding to or engaging candidates in a timely manner. As a rule, I recommend touchpoints **every one to three business days**—certainly no more than three days.

To give you a clear idea of exactly how to set the right cadence, let's break it down step-by-step using common touchpoints.

1. First, there is a **screening call** to vet the candidate and ensure there is high-level alignment. There should be a follow-up call or email, just to thank the candidate for their time, note their progress, and inform them of next steps. You can use a mix of virtual and in-person strategies.

2. Then, the candidate is introduced to different team members during a **round of two to four interviews,** depending on the size of the company, how many departments the role interacts with, and what level the role is for.

3. Between each round, there should be **touchpoints all the way to the decision to hire.** Don't let too much time pass. *One* business day can make or break whether your company gets the opportunity to hire a rockstar. Stick to the rule of one to three business days (maximum) to keep the momentum high.

One business day can make or break whether your company gets the opportunity to hire a rockstar.

It might sound crazy, but if you let that communication timeline slide, the candidate may take that delay to mean they are not being moved forward, or you risk losing them to a competitor that sees their value and expresses greater interest.

Remember, hiring is a two-way street: it is not just your decision to make, it is also the candidate's decision. That is why **every business day counts in the recruitment process.**

So, how can your team ensure that things don't slip? One effective way to maximize your timeline cadence is by setting a clear task at the end of each interaction. You want to avoid ending a screening call or interview with a vague intention to follow up. If you know you are going to move forward with this rockstar, then set up the next step during that interaction. For example, leave a cushion of five to ten minutes towards the end of the interview to allow time to coordinate and secure the next interview meeting. This will increase the likelihood that things will work in your favor as you are keeping the momentum high. Plus the rockstar is drawn to confidence in decision-making, so why not give them confidence early in the process? Ideally, concrete cadences throughout the entire process should be set within 24 hours or less.

This is another advantage of partnering with a strategic recruiter. They can act as your advocate and coordinator between each step, so you don't have to. I often have clients instruct candidates that I work with to share their feedback with me, and then I coordinate the next step. It is a type of indirect action step that takes the responsibility of timing and communication off the company's plate. As one client put it in his feedback, "A hiring and new candidate training process can be a complete time suck for myself and my team. The upfront work Rita does reduces time spent and overall frustration. My team can focus on their day-to-day roles."

Another item to keep in mind during the vetting process is extending flexibility. For example, if a company only offers interview slots on Tuesdays, then that can be a real barrier to hiring high performers. Rockstars in general are profoundly dedicated to their work—even work they are planning to leave behind. Would you expect someone like that to only be available on Tuesdays? Of course not. As the hiring company, you need to be able to pivot and accommodate candidates' schedules and obligations. I know you're busy too, but if you don't have time, *make* time! If you don't, your competitors will, and that rockstar will end up as a missed opportunity rather than a valued asset.

Be flexible in your timing to give your company the greatest chance of recruiting the best person for the job. This leads us to our next pillar of vetting and finding out who this person really is.

It's Not Just About You, It's About Them

You won't be able to find out who this candidate is unless you are learning about them on a deeper level, not just surface level, as we have discussed before. But *how* do you do that? The key is to **ask powerful questions that get them to speak about themselves, their desires, and their goals.** This is how you will get to know them as a person, which will help you assess personality fit and whether your vision *aligns* with their goals and values. As we know, alignment is the single most important factor in successful recruitment and attraction outcomes.

Why is this so valuable during the vetting process? Because the more you empower them to talk about themselves, the more you will see whether they are the rockstar aligned to your environment that you are looking for. Plus, they will feel like you care about them as a whole versus just their technical skill set. You never want a person to feel like they are on an assembly line of interviews. Hence you cannot treat interactions as mere transactions when it comes to high performers. Let's not forget, this candidate is a human being with feelings, thoughts, and goals of their own.

> *You cannot treat interactions as transactions*
> *when it comes to high performers.*

When vetting high performers, the approach needs to be different. And to feel different, it means you cannot take a checkbox approach, like we talked about in earlier chapters. Keep it fresh and keep it moving.

Best Practices for Building Rapport

The best practices for building rapport are surprisingly simple, yet they do not come naturally to everyone. This is what I call the three C's:

1. Compliments
2. Commonalities
3. Culture

Start with a Compliment

First, I always recommend starting with an acknowledgment of the candidate's accomplishments. This is a foundational premise of any successful communication as it makes the person feel seen and valued. In fact, research shows that people consistently underestimate how much of a positive impact compliments have and how much they can improve outcomes for both parties.[24] In other words, giving a compliment has a direct and measurably positive impact on relationship building, and they help the other party open up faster.

Furthermore, high performers are going to have a track record of success, and coming into a new company or new role, they will want to see that those successes will be recognized and rewarded because it indicates how future successes—at your company—will be treated. There is no need to go over the top, though. The tone should be balanced: enthusiastic but also genuine and professional.

Find and Focus on Commonalities

Commonalities lay the path for connection. This means anything you can leverage to find shared interest or mutual values, including a person's background, alma mater, or hobbies outside of work.

A great strategy is to bring in a team member who has something in common with the candidate during the interview process. Commonalities provide a comfort level that allows candidates to open up even more. The goal is to create a positive and trusting relationship from the start. You need to use every tool in your toolbox to keep a high performer engaged.

I had a memorable interaction with one candidate based on an unexpected trait we both shared. She had a passion for art. She had a minor in art history and even had created her own art collection. We developed such good rapport that she repeatedly described me as her "sounding board," as she opened up to me. Her comment made me smile as it signalled we were building trust and alignment.

Ultimately, I was able to connect her with our client, a CFO who dealt with high-net-worth individuals and their art investments. It was an instant attraction. I am very proud of that connection because it was only through those additional efforts with the candidate—the time spent hearing her more deeply and acting as a trusted advisor—that I was able to find the common link and do something great for the hiring company, as well. It often happens behind the scenes, but it's critical to sustaining a high level of success in connecting top performers with high-performing companies.

Ask Culture-based Questions

This component of rapport building should sound familiar by now, but in this section, we will dive into specifics. You know you need a candidate who is aligned with your vision and values, but how do you figure that out? How do you get to the heart of the question, *who is this person*? Asking the right questions is a little like putting the pieces of a jigsaw puzzle together.

I like to ask open-ended questions that may seem simple at first, yet often uncover deep and insightful responses. I avoid yes or no questions because the answers are clearly limited, leaving little to evaluate. The same goes for leading questions or hypotheticals given that candidates can feel unduly influenced to answer disingenuously. And if you ask standard, boring "checklist" questions, they are going to think you are a standard, boring "checklist" company.

You want to ask questions that allow the candidate to reveal who they really are in their responses. A true rockstar will have a lot to say in response to these types of questions given they are naturally reflective and analytical. They are always thinking about the future, how to improve, how they want to grow, and the kind of company that will empower them to do that. Generic responses or vague answers could reveal a lack of relevant experience or misalignment with your values.

Below, I share a few sample questions you can use if you are finding it challenging to build rapport, which will help get to that deeper level with candidates. You can use this list in your own vetting process.

And remember, be inquisitive, ask follow-up questions, and most importantly, listen!

Candidate Questions

1. *What energizes you?*
2. *Which areas do you excel in most?*
3. *What is your vision for this role?*
4. *Which responsibilities do you foresee being involved in as you continue to grow here?*
5. *What is your leadership or mentorship style?*

The goal is to identify if there is alignment within their intangibles. Tailor questions to reflect the values of your company's culture. For example, if your organization is all about disruption and innovation, ask the person to describe a time when they developed a creative solution to a problem or supported a paradigm shift in the industry. Ask about situations where they have pursued objectives in a way that reflects your environment's values.

Lastly, keep in mind that these deeper questions work best if you have successfully made a strong connection and built rapport. Candidates will be more open, honest, and relaxed, which means you will get better, more insightful responses to help in your assessment of whether or not this person is really the rockstar you want.

Diagnosing and Dealing with Misalignment

If there is a disconnect in the process, address it early and directly instead of forcing a bad fit given a bad fit will result in a bad hire. Studies show that job performance and satisfaction, as well as retention outcomes, are closely tied to person-organization alignment.[25] In fact, as much as 89% of employee turnover is caused by misalignment with organizational culture.[26]

> *As much as 89% of employee turnover is caused by misalignment with organizational culture.*

So, if you want to recruit a high performer for the long-term, you need to first identify if there is any misalignment. Building rapport will shine a light on areas where both parties are not in sync, since as a candidate gets more comfortable and starts sharing more, it can reveal disconnects between their vision and the company's. It is not a fault on either side, and it is always better to discover misalignment as early on in the process as possible. Just like in dating, if one person wants a big family and the other doesn't want kids at all, it is far better to find that out early, so both parties can move on. In a relationship, this saves heartache and regret, and in recruitment, it saves the company time and money.

Now, how do you know if a person is misaligned, and what do you do if they are? Misalignment can take as many forms as there are candidates and companies. There is a right fit for everyone, but not everyone is the right fit for every company. To paint the picture, let me share something that happened during an interview process.

There is a right fit for everyone, but not everyone is the right fit for every company.

A hiring company was interviewing a candidate they really liked, and the two parties built good rapport. The candidate, because of the trust built, was comfortable being honest. At one point in the interview, the interviewer asked, "What constructive feedback have you received from someone you report to? If your boss or manager was here, what would they tell us about you?"

"I have been told that I seem to be more of an individual contributor. I can work well in a team, but it's not my preference," the candidate replied, and he reiterated that he would rather work individually versus working in a team environment.

There is nothing inherently right or wrong about having a preference for working individually or as a team. In some roles, you need to be able to lead and work independently. In other roles, collaboration and interpersonal skills are more important. In this case, the candidate was applying for a client-facing role, which means he would be collaborating with the client and the internal team on a regular basis. While he was capable of working in a team and being successful, that preference for working individually would win out eventually, and that meant for retention purposes, this role was not the right fit for this person.

So, although the candidate's technical skill set aligned, his personality was a good fit, and his attitude towards excellence aligned with the company, this discovery represented a significant point of *misalignment*. Because of their client service environment, the company knew they could not move forward with an offer.

This story highlights the point made throughout the book of why digging deep and going beyond the basics of technical questions is so necessary. It demonstrates how building rapport can work in your favor because **misalignment can show up at unexpected times and in unexpected ways.** Identifying it early on before hiring the wrong person will save you time, effort, and resources in the long run. And this only happens when you have multiple interactions, building deeper connection with each conversation.

Building rapport works in your favor because misalignment can show up in unexpected ways. Identifying it early on will save you from hiring the wrong person.

How to Spot Red Flags

Not all rockstars are at the top of their game and beloved by all. Sometimes they're brilliant, talented, but kind of a mess, with toxic traits, not to mention a major liability.

If you are sensing red flags in the person you're recruiting, do not ignore them. I'm referring to professional or personal traits that might simply be a bad fit in almost any workplace, not just yours.

Pay attention to the details, listen to their story, and look for solid evidence of their achievements. Often, I have spotted red flags by noticing inconsistencies in a person's story or background.

I remember one time, we had a candidate in the final round of interviews. He had met with the entire team, including the CEO. During one of the last discussions, however, I noticed there was an inconsistency between what he mentioned during the interview and the story that he told me.

I am not one to jump to conclusions. I don't think it's helpful, and I always look for evidence and solid corroboration first. So, I thought, let me do my due diligence and went back to look at his resume and LinkedIn profile again. Sure enough, the timelines did not fit with his story during the interview. Was he being dishonest? It was a potential red flag, and I knew better than to ignore it.

The employment dates on his profile were in fact different. I decided to approach the candidate and have an honest discussion. We had been building rapport with this person for several weeks, so when I asked him about the inconsistencies, he opened up quickly. It turned out, he struggled with anxiety and had made several more job transitions than he listed on his resume. He said he did not want it to appear that there were too many jumps or gaps.

Now that he told me the truth, I knew what I had to do next. It was going to be disappointing to both parties yet it had to be done. The candidate had one final interview scheduled the next day, and it was very likely they would make him an offer after that.

So, I went back to our client even though it was after-hours and made them aware of the red flag we uncovered. And after reviewing this new information, they decided they could not move forward with the candidate. (Luckily, true to the law of attraction, the very next day, I connected with a different candidate who turned out to be the perfect fit for that exact role!)

Red flags can also appear in nonverbal cues and behavior. For example, if a candidate gets frustrated by the questions, it can be a sign that the person lacks patience or an inability to work well with others. It could indicate a lack of strong leadership skills because if they cannot handle the pressure of an interview, how will they handle the stresses of leadership? Or if a person appears to lack confidence, that is a red flag for communication and interpersonal skills. I have even seen candidates who do not even crack a smile during interviews—and that should certainly tell you something is off.

The Secret Weapon

Strategic recruiters have certain instincts cultivated through experience, so if you are not a recruitment expert, then your intuition on hiring high-performing talent may not be as finely tuned. Think of it like a Super Bowl-winning football coach handing over their playbook to a high school gym teacher—it will probably improve that high school team's performance, but it is only going to get them so far.

After having intimate conversations with thousands of candidates, you build a strong instinct for identifying rockstars and you gain a strong sense of when they're truly aligned with the role and the company. You start to smell BS from a mile away!

To give you an example, I was catching up with a friend, who happens to be a former Big 4 Partner, at his office in New York City. He had recently hired someone he thought was a perfect fit, but that person was significantly underperforming now that they were in the role.

"How do you know you're speaking to a rockstar?" he asked. "Do you look at what school they went to, or just their work experience?"

"That's a great question. Of course, their track record of success is a main one, not necessarily their school. It's probably not the answer you want, but most of the time it is a strong *gut* feeling," I said.

"It's funny you say that. This person we hired came from a trusted referral. She went to a prestigious tech university. Her resume was perfect. The interview was perfect. She was the ideal candidate on paper and even in-person. We even had her give a presentation in the office as part of the process (and she exceeded expectations), but she isn't producing the results we expected at all. I keep looking at her resume and back at her and wondering if this is the same person!" he said with a laugh. "It's funny you mentioned gut feeling, because I had exactly that kind of feeling—I couldn't put my finger on it, but my *gut* was telling me there was something off."

"Never go against your gut," I said. "Can I ask you a question?"

"Yeah, sure."

"When you assigned her the presentation, how much time did you give her to prepare?"

"I think we gave it to her Friday, and she came back in Monday to present," he said.

"A good tactic in the future is to only give them an hour or two to complete the case study. Since you gave her an entire weekend, she could have gotten help or had someone else put the presentation together for her. If they really know what they're doing, they can complete it within that time period. I'll bet that's what your gut was trying to tell you."

There are things you learn to look for, to sense intuitively, when you do this work professionally. I have to be excellent at what I do because my reputation is on the line with every single candidate I present. I take that to heart. My candidates are an extension of me. That's how I feel and how I approach helping my clients. Don't trust your gut, trust mine.

It's my reputation.
My candidates are an extension of me.
That's how I approach helping my clients.

A strategic recruiter is a tool you can use to increase the success rate of hiring high performers and increase the likelihood of finding someone who is aligned with your organization and who will stay with you for many years to come.

RITA'S INSIGHTS

- Keep the momentum and energy high during the interview process. Never let more than one to three business days lapse between communications.
- Building rapport is critical to assessing whether the candidate is a true rockstar. Compliments, commonalities, and culture are the key components of building rapport. Use them to your advantage!
- Never ignore red flags or signs of misalignment. Doing so will likely lead to disappointment, unmet expectations, and turnover.
- Trust your gut when making hiring decisions. If something feels off, it's off!

CHAPTER 7

INTERVIEW TACTICS THAT SEAL THE DEAL

I want to start this chapter by sharing a story of catastrophic and preventable failure. I had a rockstar candidate—a sharp, experienced leader—interviewing for a lateral position with one of my clients. I made the introduction, and the early signs were strong.

Then the hiring company made a massive, avoidable mistake.

They decided that the best person to interview this seasoned rockstar was a first-year recruiting associate who was *still in training*.

It felt like an insult to the experience and value that the candidate brought to the table, and worse, the interviewer was incapable of moving beyond basic technical questions. To her credit, the candidate handled it with grace. She explained her background clearly, trying to meet the interviewer where she was. But the trainee interviewer was totally lost. She did not have enough technical knowledge to understand the answers she was being given, and then doubled down, asking more questions along the same line, scraping the bottom of the barrel.

The worst part: there was almost no rapport built.

The interviewer was nervous, unprepared, and unqualified to understand what this rockstar was bringing to the table. And she shouldn't have been in the room to begin with.

There was no coming back from that moment. No amount of follow-up or damage control could reverse the impression left by that conversation. Why? Because *every* single interaction in the hiring process should move you one step closer to a successful outcome versus one step backwards.

The goal of this chapter is to help you increase the likelihood of that success, by optimizing that all-important but rarely mastered part of recruitment: interviewing.

We've all heard interview horror stories—a candidate shows up for what was pitched as a casual coffee chat, only to walk into a formal panel interview. Or a company representative calls once to schedule a meeting, and when the candidate misses it, they follow up with an email saying, "You must not be interested. We'll be moving on." Some of these stories are almost laughable—until you realize the damage they do. You don't want your company to be the one candidates talk about for all the wrong reasons.

Many CEOs or people in leadership positions are unaware of exactly what gets said on their behalf or their company's behalf during the interview process—and that can lead to messaging issues, lasting damage to the brand, and most importantly, missing out on great candidates who are repelled by bad experiences. Interviews are designed to help you assess candidates, yes, but they also need to be conducted in a manner that entices the best ones remain interested.

The goal is to ensure the **candidate experience is aligned with your culture and vision.** You have built the foundation, and now the interview process needs to reflect that. Without the right candidate experience, you are not going to secure the deal.

Key to this are the interactions within each step of the interview process—interactions that are the reflection of your brand and what you have built.

Without the right candidate experience, you are not going to secure the deal.

In the previous chapter, we looked at the core elements of building rapport to assess long-term alignment and fit. It was more focused on looking outward, specifically on what you need to learn about the candidate during interviews and the vetting process. Now, we are going to pivot to the qualities and skills that your advocate needs to have to be successful—whether you leverage internal HR staff, a talent acquisition team, department colleagues, or a strategic external recruiter. In this chapter, I will share advice and criteria for assessing how your team conducts interviews and related interactions, and I will provide best practices for interviewing high performers.

Basic Won't Cut It

There is a famous anecdote about an iconic hard rock band's tour rider specifying that they wanted M&Ms provided for them backstage, but with a strict provision that there must be no brown M&Ms anywhere in sight. Many people took this to mean that the band was incredibly high maintenance, yet actually, they did this to ensure that whoever was handling their rider—which included more important items like how to set up their equipment for the show—was actually paying attention and did not neglect the details. The brown M&Ms were a quick, easy way to tell how they would be treated by a particular venue and its staff. Would they be treated like rockstars, or would they be treated like anyone else walking through the door?

There is an equivalent in interviewing, and you need to roll out the metaphorical red carpet for rockstars.

The first sign you send to candidates is related to *who* you choose to conduct interviews. This person must be able to articulate your vision and values clearly in a way that truly resonates with the rockstar and builds the highest momentum possible.

Every detail matters in the interview process—starting from who is in the interview seat, their tone, and every word they say. If your team is unable to interview high performers effectively, candidates will lose confidence in the company and hesitate to proceed. Please keep this in mind! Whoever is conducting interviews needs your guidance (or delegate a team member who is competent enough to guide them) as there is a high level of sensitivity with high performers.

Every detail matters in the interview process—from who is in the interview seat, their tone, and every word they say.

The Devil Is in the Details

It might sound like an exaggeration to say that every detail matters, that one proverbial brown M&M has the potential to ruin the relationship and rapport with a rockstar candidate, but trust me, it's true. I have seen it more times than I can count. I remember one candidate, a business development leader interviewing for a head of sales role. He was sharp, bright in a way that was instantly recognizable, and a great communicator. I recommended him to a company I knew he was aligned with.

In his first interaction with their internal team member, he instantly lost all interest in the company. During the conversation, he was asking in-depth questions, but the interviewer had no capacity to answer them. Unfortunately, this person was not set up for success. They lacked the necessary knowledge to articulate the role and company in a compelling, detailed way to candidates.

Yes, it's all about the details!

When the candidate told me he had lost interest in the position, I was shocked. Prior to the interview, he was sold on the opportunity. Everything aligned. When I asked him what had changed, he said, "I just couldn't get a grasp on the role or the environment I would be in, and it doesn't give me much confidence if they can't even help me understand what I could be involved in here."

He wanted clarity, and it was nowhere to be found. Going back to the law of attraction, high performers need details, precision, and confidence throughout the process—like attracts like. How can a candidate trust a company that does not know how to explain something as basic as the responsibilities, environment, and growth opportunities? An interviewer has to be able to paint the picture, right down to the finest brushstroke details.

Optimizing Your Interviewers

There is almost certainly a gap in your organization when it comes to interviewing skills that are tailored to high performers. Let's fix this gap by asking a few questions:

1. How is your interviewer aligning your vision to the candidate's goals?
2. Are they capable of clearly communicating big picture objectives and opportunities?
3. How good are they at articulating the small details and pivoting the conversation when needed?
4. Is your team fully informed and up-to-date about short and long-term strategies that will excite a rockstar?

Since we know alignment is key to successful outcomes, the interviewer has to have a full grasp of what it is the candidate is aligning with. That means understanding both the company and the candidate on a deeper level.

A good indicator of whether they are capable of doing this is if they can answer questions in depth—even tough questions that require analysis and nuance. As we saw in the story above, this is a very important part of attracting high performers, who tend to be detail-oriented, highly analytical, and forward thinking.

High performers will want to gather as much information as they can about the company and the role through the interview process before they commit, and they are not going to ask surface-level questions. They will continuously ask specific questions that will help them assess how your company differentiates from the competition.

Is your interviewer helping rockstars see your unique selling points, or are they getting in the way by offering broad, generic answers? The interviewer should be just as prepared as the candidate before they have these conversations.

Is your interviewer helping rockstars see your unique selling points or getting in the way by offering broad, generic answers?

Equally important is the interviewer's ability to *pivot* the conversation. While there will be standard benchmarks and it is fine to use a list of questions as a starting point, interviewers have to anticipate that every conversation is going to be unique. The ability to pivot from the script means knowing when a response or a question is leading to something that can be leveraged towards alignment and influence, or conversely, when there are hints of misalignment that they can recognize and address them head on yet tactfully. It takes a high level and balance of IQ and EQ to master this skill. A box-ticking approach does not work in rockstar recruitment.

The next point of assessment can be more difficult to gauge and to teach, and this is the interviewer's demeanor. Is their tone warm and friendly or cold and closed off? Think of interviews as opportunities to create a positive, attractive impression of you and your company. We know from studies that a recruiter's demeanor has a measurable impact on candidates' perception of the hiring company, and qualities like "warmth and competence" improve hiring outcomes.[27]

Studies show a recruiter's demeanor has a measurable impact on candidates' perception of the hiring company, and qualities like "warmth and competence" improve hiring outcomes.

The goal is for the candidate to experience the interview as a conversation, not something stiff, formal, or overly preplanned. The interviewer should be able to build strong rapport and let dialogue flow naturally. This lets the rockstar's true personality shine through and nurtures rapport that leads to a close. After all, candidates are human beings, too, and if they are interviewing, it is because they are making a career move that matters a lot to them. The interviewer's demeanor should make them comfortable and confident that they are making the right move.

The last part of the assessment comes down to whether you can trust the interviewer's decision. Are they able to make good judgment calls? The person in the interview seat might have all the skills discussed above—warm demeanor, great rapport builder, the ability to pivot and answer questions in-depth, and have real insights into the company's vision—yet if they are unable to make *accurate judgement calls*, then all of that effort goes to waste.

Part of this skill comes down to *intuition*—that gut feeling we talked about in the last chapter—but part of it is a simple matter of experience. They should have a significant amount of exposure to and interactions with high-performing candidates, so they know exactly what to look for in their decision-making process. Are they able to determine if this candidate will be a reliable team member for the next three plus years? Do they know how to assess if someone is a good cultural fit?

That's another reason to consider hiring a strategic recruiting partner. As one client noted in their testimonial of Selective Insight, "Unlike other recruiting firms, Rita takes the time to get to know you, your organizational culture and what kind of leader you are. Everyone is different and she ensures the personality of the candidate would be a good match for you and your organization. She takes client service to heart and is also not afraid to have tough conversations."

So, ask yourself, is my team aware of the importance of removing the brown M&Ms?

Do your interviewers possess the ability
to make accurate judgment calls?

While most of the criteria for assessing interview skills are about positive attributes (alignment, in-depth knowledge, demeanor, judgment, etc.), there is one category that you want to avoid having in your interviewers, and that is *bias*.

It is now well-established in psychological and behavioral research that we all operate with a certain degree of implicit or unconscious bias.[28] While it is beyond the scope of this book to provide all the measures a company might take to prevent this, I can share some practical advice for assessing and avoiding interview techniques that demonstrate bias.

I once had a rockstar candidate pull out of the interview process for a role he was highly aligned with due to the bias and aggressiveness of the interviewer. The candidate was a seasoned professional with over a decade of experience, overseeing complex financial operations, managing cross-functional teams, and holding full accountability for reporting, compliance, and strategic decision-making. He had the right technical skill set along with strong leadership qualities to be successful in the role. A rockstar in every sense of the word. What he *didn't* have was experience at a big-name company—the kind of brand recognition that often opens doors, even when the skills are there.

During the course of the interview, as the candidate was talking about his experience in a mid-market firm, the interviewer would interject with negative comments like, "What did you even learn at that company?" The implication was that there was no way he could have learned as much as someone at a Big Four firm and degraded his experience because of it.

Now, aside from the fact that often there are more opportunities for learning and growth in mid-market companies given there are more responsibilities and steeper learning curves, the interviewer set a negative tone for the exchange by treating the candidate's background this way. To make matters worse, there was no warmth in the conversation. Even the interviewer's physical posture revealed a kind of aggression—she was leaning in, elbows on the table, as if it were an interrogation not an interview. Her bias totally obstructed her ability to accurately and objectively assess the candidate.

A biased interviewer is not capable of making the right judgment call and hurts your brand (this candidate ended up sharing his negative experience with his network). So, as part of your assessment, you need to ask, "Is this interviewer biased towards something?"

Next, we will discuss best practices for preparing and conducting interviews that will help your team engage with rockstars.

Engage Better

There are three things that are easy to implement and that will improve your team's ability to engage high performers and keep them interested throughout the interview stage. These are:

1. Roleplaying and Recording
2. Accountability
3. Optimizing the interview process

Again, this should be delegated to a competent team member.

The Two R's of Interviews: Roleplaying and Recording a Call

If you want to help your interviewers align talent to your vision, then you as a leader (or a competent team member who is able to effectively train others) sometimes have to pretend to be the rockstar. This is where *roleplay* can come in as an effective learning tool. It's the dress rehearsal for the big performance (the interview). The interviewer should know their marks on the stage and the lines on the page, even if it means running the scene over and over again. Test them on all the qualities and criteria discussed above. It is a process of optimization, with each practice session getting better, easier, and more natural.

For roleplaying to work, there needs to be a strong leader guiding the session. You know who you have hired, who you have fired, and who has been a good fit for your company. You have been through the process countless times, and you can spot gaps quickly. You also likely have a track record of engaging with and closing high performers, which is ideal. But since your time is limited, ensure you identify the right team member who can effectively lead this roleplay.

The ultimate test for roleplaying is *recording* a call. At the heart of this exercise is one key question: Has the interviewer had enough conversations with high performers (or roleplaying conversations) that you feel confident putting them in front of rockstars you want to close? It really all comes down to this question.

Think of it like a coach going over game film with his team. It gives you the opportunity to dig into specific moments and give them feedback on how to improve.

If you give your talent acquisition team the right playbook, then they should be able to execute with accuracy. Or, if you are sitting in on a recorded call, you can intervene and guide the process in real time. (Of course, always inform the candidate the call is being recorded for training and informational purposes.)

You may also find that an interviewer has a lot of experience conducting interviews, yet they learned their particular tactics from a previous company that does not align with yours. Different companies have different standards, and you want to ensure your brand and messaging are being promoted in the right manner. Both roleplaying and recording a call will give you real-time insights into what your team is doing and saying to people outside the organization about your brand, and will give you the opportunity to optimize and improve.

Roleplaying and recording a call will give you real-time insights into how your team is articulating your brand.

Metrics Matter

Interviews and recruitment cannot happen in a vacuum. If you want to know who the rockstars on your own team are and identify who needs more practice before they sit down in the hot seat again, then tracking results is essential. This might include setting up a dashboard to follow how many candidates a person interviews, what their success or conversion rate for hiring is, and if the candidates they suggest for hiring are retained for a certain period of time.

Accountability is especially important for anyone new to your team, even if they have experience with other companies, because it will show whether they understand how to assess alignment in candidates. Data and numbers will give you valuable feedback and help you understand the effectiveness of your recruiting methods.

Avoid Overkill

Having your interview process dialed in and fully optimized will save you time, energy, and money. If your interviewers have the skills to identify alignment and build rapport along with the intuition to identify and engage rockstar talent, then you won't need five or ten rounds of interviews, as happens in some big conglomerate corporations. You can save time by honing in early and maximizing attraction within every step—without dragging them through endless interview rounds. You want to make it easy for candidates to show you who they are and whether they align with your company, and it takes skilled, competent interviewers to accomplish that.

Excessive interviews can also lead to decision fatigue. Stakeholders involved in the process are unlikely to agree on which candidates to move forward or feel so depleted by the process that they inherently make the wrong decision. I recommend holding two to four interviews, with no more than four people total. Separate interviews are better given each interviewer can focus on a different area of expertise, whether that is technical, behavioral, leadership traits, and even administering case studies and role plays.

Best Practice Takeaways

To wind down the chapter, I'd like to share a list of best practices that will help increase success within your recruitment efforts. Some of it might seem basic, but trust me, most of it is not being done, and that is a lost opportunity.

1. *Have the right "who," the right person in the process.* This is the foundation of successful interactions throughout the recruitment process.

2. *Ensure that strong rapport is built throughout each interaction.* This is going to keep the momentum high and take the relationship to a deeper level to achieve alignment.

3. *Be explicit when you sense alignment,* meaning you should always provide feedback, especially on positive aspects of the candidate's interview. Trust me, they want to hear it! It can be as simple as, "I'm really impressed by your accomplishments. Those skills would be very valuable to our team here," or "I can see how you can make a big impact on this long-term project that will be ongoing for X-number of years." And truthfully, it's so rare that I hear a leader or an interviewer give that kind of positive, direct feedback. If you are strongly sensing that you are interviewing a rockstar and you want to move forward, yet you don't tell them, that's a lost opportunity.

4. *Don't play games, and don't lose momentum.* Often times, companies don't inform candidates of their interest immediately. If at the end of a conversation, you are confident you want to move forward, don't waste time by not telling the rockstar candidate! Schedule the next step as soon as possible. Remember, closing is happening during each interaction—including the interview stage.

5. *Bring the details to the table.* As we saw in the first story in this chapter, you cannot give surface-level answers to deep questions that rockstar candidates are asking. You may even share stories of your own—leverage success stories from within

your own organization. This is especially important if the candidate is very analytical, as many high performers are.

6. *Create a list of common questions asked by great candidates during the interview process.* Think of it like a cheat sheet for future interviews. The questions they ask are an opportunity to learn about what interests high performers most about your company. You might need to coach or guide them, yet if your team can master those questions and learn to provide deep and meaningful answers, it is going to maximize future candidate experiences. It is also a chance to get your messaging consistent across the organization.

Following these best practices will give your company a major advantage when recruiting rockstars. Interviews and interviewers are an extension of your company: your brand, your message, your image. A negative candidate experience during the interview stage—or worse, a series of bad interviews with multiple candidates—can create lasting damage to your brand. Remember, humans are hardwired to remember negative experiences more readily than good ones.[29]

So, a bad candidate experience not only affects who you get the opportunity to hire (or not), but it also tarnishes the image a successful candidate will have of your company, and it can impact people's decision to use your service. Most leaders forget that the candidates they fail to hire will end up being high-level leaders somewhere else. Now, wherever they work, you can pretty much forget about getting them as a client or customer.

A negative candidate experience during the interview stage can do lasting damage to your brand. Remember, humans are hardwired to remember negative experiences more readily than good ones.

Elite marathoners often follow the 80/20 training principle—80 percent of their training is at an easy, sustainable pace, and 20 percent at moderate to high intensity. It's how they conserve energy for the decisive push that wins the race.

In recruitment, that same push happens in the final stage when every decision, detail, and move matters most. You want this to be the set-up for a strong finish: the **Close**. Next up, we will move onto the final piece of the Build–Engage–Close™ Framework, starting with three mistakes to avoid during the close process.

RITA'S INSIGHTS

- Interviews should be intentionally structured to create a candidate experience that reflects your culture and brings your vision to life.
- Who you put in front of rockstar candidates is one of the most important decisions you make in your recruitment strategy.
- Roll out the red carpet for rockstars. Pay attention to the details, be warm and friendly, and be prepared to answer questions in depth.
- Use roleplaying and recording calls, alongside tracking performance and outcomes, to help improve interviewers' skills, specifically as they relate to engaging high performers.
- Revisit the list of best practices and proactively optimize your interview strategy. A well-equipped interview team will continue to pay dividends.

PART III

CLOSE

CHAPTER 8

HOW TO EXTEND AN OFFER THE ROCKSTAR WAY

Now, you have built the foundation and engaged the candidate through the vetting and interview process. You have made the decision that this rockstar would be a great fit for your organization, and you are ready to extend an offer. We are now in the "Close" stage of the Build–Engage–Close™ Framework.

Keep in mind, although this part is called the close process, closing was happening throughout every interaction. Your team was building momentum throughout every step, and this is the surge phase where you need to keep the momentum high right up to the finish line.

As we know, the whole process of recruiting high performers is a highly sensitive one. They will have other offers on the table, and any missteps could send them into the offices of your competition. Never assume that because things went well up to this point that closing is a done deal. You still need to put your best foot forward in this step or else risk wasting valuable time, energy, and money.

That is why this chapter begins by breaking down **three common mistakes** organizations make during the close and how to avoid them. We will take a closer look at where companies often go wrong in regards to correctly valuing high performers, the timing and approval of the offer, and who delivers the offer. In addition to guiding you through what *not* to do, we will also discuss best practices for success as you move closer to securing your rockstar candidate.

Three Mistakes to Avoid When Extending an Offer

Imagine that your team has spent the past month or more crafting a job description, screening resumes, leveraging your network to find great candidates, vetting multiple professionals during multiple rounds of interviews. And you finally find that rockstar, someone you are excited to bring onto your team, who you know will make your company better, your life easier, and your bottom line bigger.

Now, imagine all of that hard work goes down the drain because you let your guard down and fumbled the ball before the goal line. The candidate declines your offer, and you are back to square one. When this happens, it's highly demoralizing for everyone. And you *still* have an open role to fill.

Trust me, you do not want to look back on this close stage and have to ask yourself, *what could we have done differently to yield a better outcome?* The stakes are highest at the end. You have to approach the offer stage in the right manner if you want to avoid a catastrophic level of regret.

The stakes are highest at the end.

Success Is Like a Snowball—It Needs Momentum!

We've talked throughout this book about the need to keep momentum high. In the final phase, that momentum must shift into high gear.

If you've ever been mountain biking or skiing—really any sport involving speed—you know momentum keeps you stable over rough terrain. Hit the brakes, and your balance shifts forward. In an instant, you can go over the handlebars, crash into the bushes, or lose control entirely.

Momentum also helps you conserve energy and move more efficiently. The same is true in the close. When extending an offer, the more you maintain the momentum you've built, the smoother, more efficient, and more successful the close will be. Let's keep the momentum high by avoiding these **top three mistakes in the offer stage:**

1. Waiting longer than two business days to extend the offer,
2. Having the wrong person extend the offer, and
3. No communication after an offer is extended.

The number one mistake I see in the offer stage is companies waiting too long to extend the offer. This can happen for various reasons. Sometimes there is hesitation about the candidate, or maybe there is red tape that slows down the offer approval process. But remember, high performers will likely have multiple companies reaching out to them on a weekly basis. So, while you are looking to close the deal, they are being approached with other attractive opportunities from your competitors. Just like in the interview process, one business day can make all the difference between having an offer accepted or declined.

Let me give you an example to show you just how tight the timeline for success or failure can be. I remember helping one professional who was extremely interested in one of my clients, a healthcare provider. The candidate had an offer from a different company with a pretty tight deadline, but he was more aligned with my client's company and was optimistic about their offer. After the final interview with my client, everyone at the healthcare organization was on board and agreed this professional would be a great team member.

However, the CFO, who was part of the approval process, took longer than expected to approve the offer. One business day turned into two, then three, four, five days. Meanwhile, the clock was running out on the candidate's other offer. Although my client was their top choice, the candidate wanted to avoid ending up in a bad situation where they did not have any offer at all and risk ending up with no offers. There was nothing in writing. There was no security that my client would make an offer or that the other company would extend the deadline on theirs. And it was not fair to the candidate to leave them in limbo forever.

So, unfortunately, despite being the best candidate and highly aligned with my client's company, the candidate withdrew. He had lost confidence and could not afford to wait any longer. Instead, he accepted the other offer, even though it was his second choice.

I see this happen often, and there are two takeaways. First, do not allow yourself to be the bottleneck. If you are a CEO, CFO, or head of your department, you are going to have competing priorities. Think through whether you really need to be involved in the approval process, or if you feel confident in another team member to make that decision. Delaying the process, leaving candidates waiting on promises of an approved offer day after day can mean missing out on a great professional who can positively impact your team.

*As a great leader, do not allow
yourself to be the bottleneck.*

To prevent this, streamline approvals as they move through your organization, and establish clear benchmarks to keep offers from getting stuck in limbo.

The next best practice that I recommend is **getting the offer out within one to two business days** once you have made your hiring decision. Do not wait a week or two weeks. Certainly do not wait a month. Consider this a high-priority action item and maintain peak momentum. But don't just take it from me. The research supports this. Quicker offers are more likely to be accepted, and employers "benefit from accelerating their post interview job offer processes, improving their acceptance rates, and reducing vacancy times without incurring either performance or turnover penalties."[30]

While it is nice to think we are the best company and the candidate we selected is completely aligned and interested, the reality is that rockstars are being approached continuously. There is no guarantee they will accept your offer if you let the momentum die.

Extending an offer is not the same as crossing the finish line.

Remember, closing happens within every part of the process, and the candidate still needs to make a decision to accept the offer.

Another common failure I see time and time again is a lapse in communication or lack of availability between the offer and acceptance. Most of the time, candidates, especially high performers, will have a few follow-up questions. And that can be a good sign. It means they are going to be committed to their next environment and are taking the time to think through this important decision. When they think deeply, they commit deeply.

But now, your candidate is awaiting clarity. They have met multiple people within the organization. Who should they direct questions to? Did the interviewer make them feel comfortable enough to ask questions? The mistake many companies make is that no one within the company proactively offers to answer questions and be the point person. If the candidate feels hesitant or uncertain about who to follow up with, it can deflate the momentum, and that is a big risk during a very sensitive offer stage.

My recommendation is to **assign a key point of contact** to be available for questions and help successful candidates through the process. In addition to answering their questions and keeping the process moving forward, it also demonstrates what kind of organization it is. They see that there is a support system in place and their needs are being met in advance. Even better, be proactive and schedule a call to answer their questions without them having to ask first. That additional effort will close this candidate in a timelier manner and give them greater confidence in your company.

Don't Let the Wrong Person Deliver the Offer

Every senior leader has a story about landing their biggest client. Sometimes it's over a handshake in the boardroom, sometimes it's over dinner, but one thing's certain—they didn't send a junior associate to do it. When the stakes are high, the person delivering the offer *matters*.

We've talked about it many times in the book because it's one of the fundamentals of recruiting rockstars: **you must have the right person in place at each stage of the recruitment process.** And that also applies to closing. Who you choose to handle the interactions and touchpoints, and especially who you choose to extend the offer, speaks volumes about how you value and view the rockstar candidate you are trying to close.

You must have the right person in place at each stage when recruiting a rockstar.

In Chapter 6, we talked in-depth about the importance of building rapport and how to do it. By the Close stage, you (or someone in your organization) have built a relationship with this high performer. Why not use that momentum to increase the likelihood of securing the deal? Work smarter, not harder. Leverage all that effort you put in through the Build and Engage stages to seal the deal.

Remember, closing is highly sensitive. It's a huge decision for this rockstar. Let's put ourselves in their shoes. They are thinking of committing to one company for several years or more. They are contemplating the trajectory of their career and their life. So how can you help? We all know trust helps secure deals more quickly. Studies show that organizations should carefully manage communications at this stage in order to reduce uncertainty and improve recruitment outcomes. Who communicates an offer and how that offer is communicated impacts how a candidate perceives their future relations within the organization.[31] Again, it comes down to relationships and your ability to leverage them in your favor.

> *Who communicates an offer and how*
> *that offer is communicated impacts*
> *how a candidate perceives their future*
> *relations within the organization.*

Lastly, it is critical that the offer stage not turn into a mere *transaction*. What do I mean by this? If you bring in someone who was not part of the interview process to extend the offer, it is going to signal a box-ticking exercise. It will seem impersonal and even worse, make it seem as if the people who the candidate spent time with, trusts, and has good rapport with cannot be bothered to finalize the deal.

Yes, it's business, but business is personal, too. And rockstars expect to be treated with the respect they deserve. They don't want to feel like a commodity, especially not when they are in this late stage.

The offer should be personalized, an extension of the relationship formed through the Build and Engage stages. Think about who in your organization has built the greatest rapport with the candidate. Who would have the most influence? Who is the most meaningful or impactful person who could extend the offer in the candidate's eyes? Put *that* person in the driver's seat and hit the gas.

Don't Undervalue High Performers

Money is not everything, but it isn't *nothing* either. High performers know their worth. They will drive exceptional ROI and accelerate your organization's growth. If you undervalue a rockstar in the offer stage, you risk undermining the entire relationship. Rockstars are dedicated, passionate people who want to give their time, energy, and expertise to amplify your brand and increase your success. You wouldn't make a lowball offer on a prime penthouse and expect the seller to take you seriously. Similarly, offering a high performer a salary package below fair market value can instantly diminish their interest and trust.

I remember one client of mine that was highly interested in finding a rockstar from the investment banking world. Their organization was not an investment bank itself, but they knew that professionals with exposure to that industry fit the mold of who they were looking to hire. I found a candidate who aligned with their organization and everything they wanted for the role.

The company was excited to secure this exceptional candidate and was eager to extend an offer. But they failed to do their research on the market value for a professional with his background.

Now, if you know anything about investment banking, you already know that people aren't drawn to that industry because it's a fun, low-key job. For the most part, it's for the money! The client came in with an offer way below fair market value—to the tune of $20,000 lower. Needless to say, the candidate was shocked. He probably would have been insulted if he weren't so incredibly surprised.

He and I had built great rapport, and he reached out to me asking if he had done something wrong during the interview process to warrant such a low offer. Thankfully, I was able to mediate between my client and the candidate to smooth the waters and secure the deal, along with an offer in line with market value. They had misread his interest and alignment as willingness to settle for less than he was worth, but rockstars do not settle, even if their motives are not strictly financial. Had I not stepped in and thoughtfully maneuvered the situation, the candidate would have likely walked away without a second thought.

Our expertise in this aspect of recruiting has been hugely beneficial to many of our clients. As one client remarked, "Selective Insight advised us on appropriate compensation levels, what top candidates are looking for in a company (culture, benefits, opportunities) and provided advice on current market conditions to 're-set' our expectations. This advice ensured we closed key candidates quickly and ensured they stayed with us long-term."

In the next chapter, we will talk about negotiation strategies, but for now, it is sufficient enough to know that grossly undervaluing high performers is generally a huge mistake and can lead to a negative recruitment outcome. At minimum, part of your diligence process needs to include researching fair market value for the role and level you are recruiting for.

Go the Extra Mile

Have you ever stayed at a hotel that pulled out all the stops for you? Champagne and chocolates in the room on arrival, breakfast basket with fresh pastries and local jams, or customized gifts that make you feel seen and welcome. If you're a loyal customer, a top-of-the-line hotel will even add personal touches in accordance with your preferences. (If you've stayed at the Four Seasons, then you know what I am referring to.) Without going over the top, this is the level of personalization that can help close a rockstar.

Little nudges, tiny action steps can keep the momentum high, reignite the excitement, and push candidates who are still deliberating on an offer towards your favor. It can be as simple as calling or emailing (but calling is much better!) to say congratulations on the offer, especially if that call is from someone who they met with in a leadership or C-suite position. Explicitly tell the rockstar you are excited for them to potentially join your company. Those words mean a lot. Hearing from the hiring company can strengthen a candidate's desire to accept an offer and encourage them to accept more quickly. It can be deeply motivating and reassuring.

I have seen this work firsthand. The CEO was involved in the interview process and recognized the talent in this one high performer. He was so intent on securing this candidate that he took it upon himself to call, congratulate him on the offer, and made himself available to answer any questions.

Now, let's put ourselves in the candidate's shoes. How would you feel if the CEO, Board Member, or Founder of a hiring company called you personally?

It turned out, that one small gesture made it an easy decision, and the candidate accepted within the same day.

It sounds basic, but a nudge goes a long way as it reassures the candidate of your high interest in their value and shows you respect their decision. Many companies assume breakdowns only occur because of something significant, but more often, it is a very small detail like this that causes a deal to fall apart. Why is that? Because another company is calling them, is congratulating them, and is making them feel warm and welcomed.

Companies assume that breakdowns only occur because of something significant, but more often, it is a small detail that causes a deal to fall apart.

Let's walk through a couple of other tactics you can use to seal the deal. If you're serious about a candidate, consider setting up a casual in-person meeting—coffee or lunch can go a long way.

Another effective approach is organizing a meet-and-greet event where your top performers connect with the rockstar you're pursuing.

These small, strategic gestures go the extra mile and make the candidate feel genuinely valued. When candidates feel special, attraction and momentum stay high, bringing you one step closer to a successful close.

In one case, the company knew they were up against tough competition and wanted to stand out. They hosted a company-wide event and invited the candidate to attend. It gave the candidate a chance to meet future team members, experience the culture firsthand, and connect beyond the formal interview setting. It also signaled how highly the company valued them—keeping momentum high post-offer.

One caveat is that you don't want to put too much pressure on the rockstar candidate, so you can present it as a normal social event without telling them that it was organized specifically for them. (Don't be that clingy, over-eager person who gifts someone a pair of expensive emerald earrings on the second date.) Yet strategies like this yield amazing results!

And while connection is key, **so is follow-through.**

If a candidate is excited to start earlier than your planned date, take the steps needed to make it happen. That extra effort shows you're just as invested—and it can be the final push they need to commit.

As we know, rockstars are in high demand and low supply. For that reason and that reason only, you need to prioritize any action steps that will help secure them, including the decision to hire, approvals, formal offer, and any follow-up steps leading to acceptance.

Let's wrap up this chapter with a few reminders:

1. Do not sleep on an offer. Go with your gut.
2. Have a structured process and strategic plan for the offer phase. Put a cap on how many people are involved in the approval process and a time limit for how long it takes.
3. Have the right person in place to make the offer. Make it personal. Make it meaningful. Walk them through the details and be open to answer questions.
4. Schedule a follow-up call in the next one to three business days. And keep the momentum high with personalized touchpoints.

This is what a successful offer process looks like!

RITA'S INSIGHTS

- The three most common mistakes during the offer stage are: (1) waiting too long to extend an offer, (2) having the wrong person communicate the offer, and (3) extending such a low offer that it undervalues the rockstar's true worth.
- An offer is a *big* decision for high performers and a highly sensitive stage of the recruitment process. Keep the momentum high, and be aware that every gesture influences the rockstar.
- Leverage the relationship you have built throughout the recruiting process to make rockstar candidates feel seen, welcomed, and valued.
- So often, it is a very small detail that causes a deal to fall apart! Don't let that detail be the reason your offer gets rejected.

CHAPTER 9

HOW TO NEGOTIATE LIKE AN EXPERT

Leonardo da Vinci's *Salvator Mundi* sold for a record-breaking $450.3 million in 2017. It is a priceless work of art, and yet, there comes a point where someone *has* to put a price on it. There are two questions that help determine this: what is it worth to *you,* and what will *not* having it cost you?

Negotiations are a highly strategic and a highly sensitive topic in business. In the case of negotiating with a rockstar candidate, you need to think of it like closing the deal on a priceless work of art. This is something rare and valuable that will continue to increase in value and add ROI to your company for many years to come. Yes, you have to put a price on it, but like a great work of art, it is about so much more than money, and saying or doing the wrong thing might mean you lose the opportunity to secure this incredible, one-of-a-kind person for your team.

This chapter is all about the delicate—and some say dreaded—dance of negotiations. But it is not something you need to tiptoe around or feel like you're strapping on armor and preparing for battle.

If you have followed the Build–Engage–Close™ Framework so far, then you have set yourself up for success in the negotiation stage. In this chapter, I will walk you through why you should avoid the old model of adversarial negotiations and instead **leverage alignment for a frictionless process.** I will offer tools and advice on how to respond if a candidate has another offer—and how to strategically guide and influence them to join your organization organically. And lastly, I will share proven solutions that have consistently helped my clients overcome common sticking points during this part of closing.

Winning with Alignment

Negotiations are often popularly depicted as adversarial, especially in the media, and it does make for good television. The candidate wants to squeeze the company for every dollar and perk they can swing, and the company wants to pay as little as they can to preserve their bottom line. But this is not a divorce between a warring couple feuding over who gets the house and who keeps the dog. This is the start of something great, the culmination of all those touchpoints, "dates," and deep interactions.

You have spent all this time building a relationship, creating rapport, and finding alignment—let it work for you! I always advise clients to view negotiations as collaborative rather than adversarial. Seek a win-win solution by leveraging alignment rather than trying to "best" the other party.

In truth, the best negotiation does not feel like a negotiation at all. When you have followed the steps laid out in the Build–Engage–Close Framework thus far and kept the momentum high throughout the entire process, then the negotiation to secure this rockstar becomes much easier, and you are one step closer to closing.

The best negotiation does not feel like a negotiation at all.

In a best-case scenario, there may be such natural alignment between the high-performing candidate and your organization that there is very little to negotiate. If a candidate has all the information they need, this part of the process is just filling in the final details of the offer to seal the deal. Ideally, that is the space you want to be in.

But not every situation will land in this ideal place, so it's important to be prepared for every scenario. Here's **how to approach an offer negotiation**:

1. Leverage influence, not aggressive tactics.
2. Reemphasize the alignment that already exists.
3. Fully listen to the desires of the candidate.
4. Extend flexibility where it makes sense.
5. Add urgency when needed.

In addition to expert advice derived from actual professional experience, we will also apply insights and approaches from Chris Voss, former FBI negotiator and author of *Never Split the Difference,* which have been battle-tested and used in a range of situations, including recruitment negotiations.

Use Influence, Not Aggression

First, do not try to bargain or be aggressive. Some recruiters use "bargaining" and "negotiating" interchangeably, but they are very different. Bargaining is transactional. Just like we wanted to avoid creating a transactional relationship in the Engage phase, we want to continue to avoid it during the Close phase of the framework. Bargaining is part of the old adversarial mindset. It means exchanging one thing for another, being pushy or aggressive about what *you* want, and trying to create a winning situation only for yourself. That is going to repel a high performer, which is the last thing you want at this stage. More importantly, bargaining and transactional relationships are not how real influence works.

Real influence in negotiations requires the art of finding alignment and using it to achieve the best outcome for both parties. This does not mean you have to give into every one of the candidate's requests or requirements. It means using the rapport you have built to understand what is driving the candidate's decision-making process and using that knowledge to steer them towards an outcome that aligns with both your goals. It is about shifting the conversation to a deeper level and using influence to close. As Voss discovered, "Persuasion is not about how bright or smooth or forceful you are. It's about the other party convincing themselves that the solution you want is their own idea. So don't beat them with logic or brute force. Ask them questions that open paths to your goals."[32]

The reason this matters is because there is a direct correlation between how a person feels they were treated during recruitment and negotiation—and their long-term retention.[33] The research is clear: candidate experience directly impacts employee loyalty. One such study concluded that, "Specifically, job negotiation interactional justice perceptions have a lingering effect on an individual's turnover intentions."[34] If an employee feels they were treated unfairly, pushed too far in negotiations, or forced to concede too much, then they are more likely to leave the company sooner—and then you are back to square one.

There is a direct correlation between how a person feels they were treated during recruitment and negotiation—and their long-term retention.

The best approach is to have someone in place who can reemphasize alignment and guide the candidate towards an outcome that benefits you both. More often than not, this eliminates the need to even have a negotiation discussion. **Both sides win when what matters to the candidate naturally aligns with what your company offers.**

What's on the Table?

A true rockstar is more than a resumé, more than a number on your payroll, and more than a dollar amount on a piece of paper. That means there has to be more to the negotiation than money. Continue the rapport by reemphasizing the **alignment**. This is where what you have *built* as part of your attraction engine—the culture, environment, branding, leadership, everything we talked about in Part I—really kicks into high gear. These foundational aspects of your company are what *attract* high performers and what will help close them.

Typically, with high-performing professionals, what interests them most during negotiations is not the money. It is the high-growth potential of the opportunity as a whole, intellectual and professional stimulation in their day-to-day, and sometimes flexibility with respect to having a hybrid working arrangement.

The best thing you can do during an offer negotiation is to **re-emphasize the alignment of what is most important to them as an individual and what your company has to offer**, whether that is the opportunity to do interesting work that continuously challenges them, to be mentored by a leader higher up in the organization, or to be fast-tracked to the next level without a tenure mark.

You can pay a rockstar highly competitive compensation, but if they are doing repetitive, boring work that does not excite them or allow them to progress in their career, then they are not going to be happy. And eventually, they are going to land a more interesting job with the same compensation at another company. I have seen it happen many times where companies have tried to downplay the lack of alignment with a big pay package. No one wins in that situation. The company does not achieve sustainable ROI from the hire, and the employee does not achieve any fulfillment from their new role.

You might recall the managerial candidate from Chapter 6 who was deciding between two offers—one with a client of mine and one with another company. I still vividly remember the call when I reeled him back in. It was during the COVID pandemic, and I was outside walking with my daughter and husband when my phone rang.

"Hey, it's me," the managerial candidate said. "I have another offer, and it's very competitive."

"Okay, let's discuss it," I said. I covered the phone with my hand, turned to my husband, and whispered, "Sorry, I need to take this."

I spent the next half hour in the parking lot, walking back and forth, going over every detail with the candidate. The competing offer was an additional $15,000 over the base salary my client was offering, but I knew the candidate's goals, and I wanted to make sure he was aware of what he was getting himself into if he accepted the other offer.

"I recall that you mentioned what's most important to you is work-life balance," I said. "That company, that role is not going to give you what you want. You're going to be on call 24-7. They might call you on a Saturday and expect you to fly out and travel on Sunday—not as an exception but as a requirement."

"Really?"

"Yes. And I remember you mentioned you're planning to grow your family and how important your family time is to you. Think about how all that travel and those long hours are going to impact that quality time. Isn't that worth more than the money they're offering? Think about what you have to give up for the additional compensation."

It was an "aha!" moment for him that shook him out of what I like to call *shiny object syndrome*, when candidates get distracted by a big pay offer—when what they really want is to do meaningful work for an exceptional company and still have most of their weekends.

"Rita, thank you. This is a no-brainer, actually. I'm not going to accept that other offer," he told me.

When I'm advocating for my client and I know there's better alignment with my client than with a competing company, that is where real influence is everything. There is no need to spin the truth or exaggerate. I just present the facts and re-emphasize the alignment, and it also helps that I have deep business knowledge. I know what is going on in other companies and how they operate. I have a bird's eye view of the industry thanks to my vast network and my experience as a career coach, which works in my client's favor.

So, when we talk about negotiations, it is up to you to clearly articulate the details of what is on the table and how it aligns with what is most important to the rockstar (which you learned during the vetting process). Obviously, this includes salary but also growth potential, strategic responsibilities of the role, and any unique aspects of your organization that align with what is most important to the rockstar.

We just went through a few things that we can control in the negotiation process. Often though, if you are part of a structured organization, then there is going to be limited flexibility with big ticket items like salary, annual bonus targets, and PTO—and so it remains critical that you continue to re-emphasize the items that are most important to the rockstar.

If you have built strong rapport with the candidate, like we have talked about throughout the book, you should already know what that is, but if not, do not be afraid to ask them directly. "What is most important to you in this offer?" or "How do you feel about this offer?" are great openers to start negotiations.

The more information a negotiator has about a candidate, the more effective their strategies and influence become.

This is also where having an external recruiter can be a huge advantage. Candidates are more likely to open up to a trusted third party than to the hiring company wooing them about what they want and any concerns—especially if that party has built up strong rapport, trust, and communication throughout the process. In a survey of experienced negotiators, researchers found that "preparation and planning skill" ranked as the most important trait of an effective negotiator.[35] According to the survey, the more information a negotiator has about a candidate, the more effective their strategies and influence become.

As a strategic recruiter, the role is to advocate and influence. During negotiations, it's about articulating and highlighting the points that matter most to the candidate—beyond just compensation. This means painting a clear picture of what accepting the offer would look like for them, and sometimes, for their families. By maintaining the same warmth and openness shown throughout the process, candidates feel comfortable asking questions and seeking guidance as they make their final decision. It's an opportunity to fill in the details and reinforce the alignment that already exists between the candidate and the hiring company.

As we also learned, the recruiter's demeanor and behavior impact candidates' perception of the hiring company. The same effect has been demonstrated during the negotiation phase. In a study on personality and negotiation performance, researchers at Western Washington University concluded that the negotiator's agreeableness and openness positively impact their outcomes, in large part because they are better able to gather information about a recruit's motives and "use their in-depth understanding to create persuasive arguments."[36] Again, I cannot reiterate enough that *who* you put in place at every stage in the recruitment process matters significantly. It has measurable effects on the success of your hiring process and, ultimately, the success of your business!

Now, there is a big challenge that inherently lies within your own team. Advocates who are internal to your company are capped in their influence because candidates view them as biased towards their own company. In contrast, a trusted strategic recruiting partner is seen as more neutral. Their role isn't to convince a candidate to accept a role that doesn't align with their goals—because what's not in the candidate's best interest ultimately isn't in the company's best interest either. And placing the wrong person in the wrong role serves no one. That sense of neutrality and alignment builds mutual trust and **trust is what influences top candidates to commit**.

This also relates back to our discussion in Chapter 5 and how sales tactics can be applied to recruitment. As you will recall, the best salespeople are not pushy or aggressive. They do not try to convince someone to buy something they do not want or need. As the saying goes, "He who has learned to disagree without being disagreeable has discovered the most valuable secret of negotiation"—a principle reinforced by negotiation experts like Chris Voss.[37]

He who has learned to disagree without being disagreeable has discovered the most valuable secret of negotiation.

Instead, the best salespeople highlight the alignment and shared desire that is already present. Be intentional about how you position your offer—reiterating the alignment of growth, leadership development, and uniqueness of your company.

It is worth noting here that negotiations are also an opportunity for you to continue to assess the candidate's demeanor. If a candidate suddenly becomes aggressive and unrelenting during this stage, consider it a red flag because a true rockstar does not communicate in that manner. It may also indicate how they are going to behave once they join your organization. Is this a sign of how they are going to treat others? Great leaders lead with a softer, more intentional approach. They remain open-minded, ask for flexibility when needed, and don't rely on drawing hard lines or using aggression to get results.

The Goldilocks Zone

As mentioned at the start of the chapter, rockstars are a valuable asset, and, well, there has to be a number attached to that value. So, how do you make an offer that appeals to a high performer without undercutting your bottom line? The goal is to find the "Goldilocks Zone." If you remember the fairytale of *Goldilocks and the Three Bears*, you will recall that each time Goldilocks tries something that belongs to the bears—their porridge, their chairs, even their beds—the first is too much, the second too little, but the third is always "just right." This is what you are aiming for with your offer—only you want to get it right the first time rather than making mistakes through trial and error as Goldilocks did.

My advice to you is to offer, at minimum, slightly above fair market value. Why? Because if you come in at just fair market value, then it tells the candidate that you are just an average organization offering an average salary—and no rockstar wants to be seen as settling for average. Your company is exceptional, so why should your compensation package be anything but?

Now, keeping in mind the Goldilocks Zone, making an offer above fair market value does not mean going to the extreme high end and offering a starting salary that is excessive. If the difference between expectation and offer is in the range of $5,000 to $10,000, then that typically is reasonable and there is flexibility to negotiate.

I do recommend having a slightly bigger cushion for the *right* candidate though as they will do their research and see other competitive offers in the marketplace.

Again, this is another area where a strategic recruiting partner can give you an edge in negotiations. In a study on the psychological factors involved in negotiations between candidates and hiring organizations, researchers found that, "Internal organizational agents who negotiate starting salary packages with job applicants may not always act in the organization's best interests."[38] Indeed, they found that internal agents, meaning HR staff or talent acquisition teams, impact final negotiation outcomes on everything from hiring, salary size, to applicant—in ways that may oppose the interests of the organization they represent.

"Internal organizational agents who negotiate starting salary packages with job applicants may not always act in the organization's best interests."

In contrast, clients often seek our guidance during negotiations, recognizing the value of an objective perspective grounded in deeper insight into what the candidate wants and how they align. Questions like "What do you feel is a competitive offer here?" or "How do our internal benchmarks compare?" come up frequently. While the specifics vary by organization, the goal remains the same: make informed, compelling offers that attract top talent—and that's where strategic guidance makes all the difference.

If the Build–Engage–Close Framework has been followed throughout the recruiting process, then you should have already gathered some information about salary expectations. Likewise, this means your advocates were at least somewhat transparent about the company's compensation structure during the vetting and interview process. Do not wait until the offer stage to assess whether both parties are on the same page regarding compensation.

You might recall the story from Chapter 8 about a great candidate who went through the whole recruitment process and successfully landed an offer with my client. Everyone who interviewed this candidate loved him, even the CEO who met with him in the final round yet the company made an offer that was $20,000 below fair market value—and did not align with the candidate's expectations. Now, let us look at that example through a negotiating lens.

We can see from what we have learned in this chapter that the company started with too much of a cushion. When they realized this candidate had another competitive offer on the table, the company immediately increased the salary by $20,000 to fill the gap. It nearly cost them the perfect candidate, and the entire mismanaged offer process could have been easily avoided.

Luckily, I stepped in to maneuver and influence the process, and as a result the company secured the candidate. The point is that you want to do everything in your power to avoid these missteps because you might not be able to bring it back from the brink of collapse. Lowballing jeopardizes not only the possibility of recruiting a rockstar—if done repeatedly, it could tarnish your brand.

Imagine you're finalizing a merger. Every term has been discussed, the lawyers are ready, and then, in the final minutes, the other side drops in a brand-new demand that changes the economics entirely.

You'd feel blindsided and probably walk away. Compensation works the same way. The offer should never be a surprise at the end. Now, money is not always the most important thing to a high-performing professional, but at the end of the day, everyone works for money, and we have to ensure that expectations align with what your company can actually offer. In my experience, greater transparency leads to greater success. That is what leads to the best outcome—finding that "just right" Goldilocks Zone without wasting time and energy on trial and error.

Greater transparency leads to greater success.

How to Handle Competing Offers

As we have noted throughout the book, a real rockstar has multiple offers coming across their desk every single day. This may seem like a problem at this stage in the process, but remember, this also validates their value, skill, and expertise. So, how do you make sure that *your* offer is the one they choose?

If the candidate has another offer, the first action step is to find out whether your company is their first choice. This can be as simple as asking the candidate directly or using a strategic recruiter to do some due diligence on your behalf. The reason this is such an important piece of information is that if your company is not their top choice, then you may want to pull back on putting in additional efforts to secure them. Conversely, just because they have another offer (or multiple offers) does not mean they are seriously considering it. You need to know where you stand before you can proceed.

If your company *is* their first preference, then there are several ways to use influence to close them. Again, gather as much information about the competing offer as you can. As Voss writes, "Negotiation is not an act of battle. It's a process of discovery. Your goal is to uncover as much information as possible."[39] Most of the time, candidates are willing to share this because they can use the other offer to get your company to match what is being offered elsewhere. It may be that the other company is offering a higher compensation package and includes an additional detail that is exciting to them, too.

Is there any flexibility in your own offer? Is there room to match the competing compensation package? Oftentimes, it's not feasible to match a competing offer that significantly exceeds fair market value, so then you need to assess what other factors can excite or influence the candidate and put in additional efforts right away.

Don't play hardball. You're not dealing with the average candidate. High performers do not like to play games when it comes to the future of their careers. Do not bat numbers back and forth. It can make your organization appear inexperienced or indecisive, and the longer it takes to finalize the deal, the more likely the candidate will walk away or accept another offer. Remember, **how a candidate is treated during negotiations has a direct correlation to their retention.** So, even if there is alignment and even if the candidate does choose to accept your offer, if they feel like they were treated poorly or their hand was forced during this stage, it can mean shaving off years from that ROI.

So, what is a successful tactic that can help expedite the negotiation? One strategy is to apply gentle pressure by adding a sense of urgency to the next steps. If there's room for negotiation and the candidate is asking for more—whether it's compensation or additional benefits—urgency can help move the conversation forward in a way that benefits both sides.

For example, let's assume your company offered $170,000 and left a cushion of $5,000 to $10,000 on the base salary. Now, imagine the candidate is asking for flexibility and says, "I really would love to join your company, and I would accept your offer if it was at $180,000." You know you have that cushion, and you know this is a rockstar candidate. You have no reservations. My advice would be to first let them know you are willing to go the extra mile for them by replying with, "We are going to need an additional approval for this increase, and it will take additional efforts." Then, if you get that approval, apply gentle pressure through creating a sense of urgency: "We're going to increase your offer to $180,000 base, but we need a response by end of day today."

Sprinkling in some urgency as a negotiating tactic is highly effective. Why does that tactic work so well? It shows the candidate that you are willing to make additional efforts, that you value them and want to meet their needs, and that you are capable of acting in a timely manner—all of which reflects positively on the organization as a whole. If the candidate is excited about your company, they'll view the exchange as a positive step toward getting what they wanted—rather than pressure. It increases that excitement, keeps the momentum high, and often becomes the final piece that helps close the candidate quickly.

How to Get High Performers Off the Fence (and into Your Office)

I see it all the time. A company spends weeks or months going through resumes, vetting and interviewing candidates, finding a high performer who aligns perfectly, only for the momentum to run out and progress to stall at the negotiation stage.

We've seen multiple clients who went through this exact process, made an offer, and gave the candidate three business days to decide. Three days passed, and the candidate requested more time. The hiring company agreed but never set a new deadline. One week ran into two. Two weeks dragged into three. They maintained touchpoints, but by now they had drifted into uncertain territory.

Each business day that passed decreased the likelihood of acceptance. And each day was one more day that critical role was left empty—draining momentum, delaying impact, and silently costing the company in ways that compound over time. The longer they left it open, the more likely that their second and third choice candidates would also drop off and accept other offers. It was nearly a month before the candidate declined the offer, and the company was back to its original starting point.

If you are a sports fan, there is nothing like a close game or race to keep you on the edge of your seat. But as much as we all love a tiebreaker just before the buzzer in basketball or a winning Hail Mary play in football, a nail-biting finish is not what any of us are hoping for when we are trying to close. If you remember the New York Jets under Rex Ryan in the 2009 and 2010 seasons, you know how many games came down to the final seconds—a thrilling way to win in sports, but a risky way to operate when you're trying to close a deal. In recruitment, getting a rockstar candidate over the line sometimes takes just the right move. Here are three strategies to achieve that winning outcome.

We know that high performers seek long-term challenging opportunities and continuous skill development. So, strategy number one is to take the opportunity to back up your promises for growth. Create a projection plan for them that shows where they can be in one, three, and five years to help them visualize the fast track you have proposed to them. I have clients that may even mention how the compensation package grows alongside the growth in their role as they progress to higher levels.

Second, if the negotiations are dragging on too long, offer a sign-on bonus attached to a specific start date. Let's say you have already given them the best practice of three business days to consider and respond. If they come back after three days and request more time or try to negotiate further, then you have hit a sticking point. Leveraging a sign-on bonus incentivizes a timely decision in your favor.

Better yet, have a standard policy for how many business days you allow to extend offers. That way, when you communicate with candidates, they have a clear idea of the timeframe they have to make a decision. I often see clients keep the window open for too long, and then they lose candidates. It gives them too much time to lose momentum with your company and consider offers from others.

Third, one strategy that consistently accelerates decisions with top candidates is the use of visuals. Most high performers are highly analytical. They want proof, not promises. Providing internal data, performance metrics, or a visual roadmap of their potential career progression can make a critical difference. It builds immediate confidence in the opportunity, helps them envision their long-term growth within your organization, and reinforces the value of the work they'll be contributing to from day one. When a candidate can see a clear, exciting future laid out in front of them, they move forward faster—and with greater confidence.

Ultimately, it is important to remember that the rockstar candidate you are negotiating with is making a commitment to your company for years to come. It is best to keep it simple, come to the table with a great offer, remind them of all the ways you are in alignment, and give them a clear timeline for deciding. Do that, and you are sure to close your rockstar!

In the next chapter, we will discuss what to do to ensure you retain this great talent and maximize the long-term ROI of your recruitment efforts.

RITA'S INSIGHTS

- Negotiations are not a battle to be won by one side. Leverage rapport and alignment to secure a win-win outcome for you and the candidate.
- Consistently important in every stage of the recruitment process, *who* you use to negotiate for your company has a direct effect on the outcome. Make sure it is someone who knows how to pivot, deeply understands the candidate's goals, and will represent your best interests.
- If a candidate is on the fence or has multiple offers, first, confirm whether you are their top choice. Then, look for a reasonable middle ground that demonstrates flexibility without compromising your standards or values. (And communicate clearly to the candidate how far you're willing to go to secure them!)
- *Do* use urgency to gently nudge them towards a timely decision. *Don't* be pushy or aggressive.
- For top talent, the promise of career progression and fast-tracking often outweighs even the most competitive compensation. Don't shy away from reemphasizing this key aspect as it will help you close the rockstar faster.

CHAPTER 10

RETAINING ROCKSTARS FOR MAXIMUM ROI

A good friend of mine, a leader in the fintech space, mentioned to me a disaster story about a recent hire in his department. Their talent acquisition team spent months recruiting an exceptional high performer. The new employee was highly motivated, driven, and aligned. And then to my friend's shock and disappointment, he left within three months of being hired.

"Why do you think that happened?" I asked. "What's your onboarding process like? Who did you connect him with once he was in the office?"

"What do you mean?" he asked. "He was so well-aligned, I just thought he would mesh and figure it out once he was there."

As it turned out, after the initial meet and greets, there was no formal process to integrate or recognize the new employee. There was no clear communication from leadership about the impact this person will have on the organization and its goals. The new hire was left to settle into his desk and basically felt invisible. The rest of the team had no idea how it would impact the organization or, perhaps more importantly, them as individuals.

No formal onboarding process meant retention was at high risk and there was a high probability of losing the rockstar. Yet what you don't want to do is have a generic 90-day onboarding process as that is not the best fit for high performers.

This chapter is designed to help you improve your onboarding process, **set the tone to gain buy-in from the rest of your team**, and build on the warmth in the relationship that attracted and engaged the rockstar in the first place. I will share easy to implement, low or no cost strategies for a big impact on retention, productivity, and employee satisfaction. I will also give you tips on how to minimize burnout that can lead to attrition.

Get Everyone on Board with Onboarding

At minimum, every successful organization needs a clear onboarding roadmap to help new hires navigate the first days or weeks in a new role and environment. This may include readily available training materials and making formal introductions with the new hire's key points of contact. Take the time to make meaningful introductions to colleagues who they will collaborate with on a regular basis *and* key leaders in different parts of the organization.

Depending on where everyone is located, you may choose to make these introductions in a group setting or individually, virtually or in-person. If you want to go the extra mile, schedule a breakfast or lunch to help the new hire warm up to the environment and give them the opportunity to get to know others in a more relaxed, social setting. It is a great chance to build relationships faster, and *better relationships yield better outcomes.*

Whichever option you choose, these introductions should go beyond a quick hello where all they have time to exchange are names and job titles. That is not going to make anyone feel connected. Why does it matter? Because meaningful formal introductions, especially with key leaders and team members, will de-risk pushback. Without buy-in in any organization, processes will move slowly and relationships may even collapse.

Meaningful formal introductions, especially with key leaders, will de-risk pushback. Without buy-in, processes will move slowly and relationships collapse.

It is all too common for veteran leaders who are "set in their ways" to be resistant to change, particularly if they are fixed-mindset leaders. So, when a rockstar joins an organization to drive transformation and to add value quickly, it can sometimes ruffle feathers.

Thus, part of the onboarding process has to incorporate proactively securing *buy-in* from the rest of the team. A great way to ensure that high performers are met with warmth and acceptance is to clearly communicate expectations and roles from the beginning. It can be as simple and direct as, "This person is here to add value to X process to make our lives easier." Perhaps give a nod to some of their previous achievements. That kind of clear, concise, and *warm* communication can motivate collaboration, improve the probability of success, and make it possible for them to have a significant impact more quickly.

To take it one step further, communicate how the rockstar's contributions can benefit other people in the organization personally. For example, if the new hire is going to help with an upcoming acquisition by creating strategic financial models that will increase visibility into the organization, or if they are in business development and are going to leverage relationships to help grow the company, then that means more revenue for the company. And increased revenue means higher bonuses and growth opportunities for everyone. Help them connect the dots between the rockstar's value and the value they can derive from it.

Ensure you are also being explicit about the win-win. That will provide your new rockstar the authority and respect to implement changes and effectively manage team members. It is a critical component to securing buy-in.

On the other hand, if you do not explicitly discuss expectations, then other employees have no choice but to fill in the blanks for themselves—and their perception may be off. It can make the start of the new hire's integration more difficult if they constantly have to explain themselves and fight for authority early on. Of course, rockstars want to be strategic and they like to be challenged, but not in this way—not with pushbacks that interfere with execution.

Another component that is helpful is making the new hire aware of common challenges in your environment to avoid surprises. You do not want to blindside this rockstar. High performers will be highly aware that there are all different types of people in an organization. Nothing is going to be perfect, and they do not expect it to be. Still, you want to set them up for success by informing them of any existing issues either within the organization or with external partners.

For example, if certain leadership styles are more effective with certain team members, then they will know to pivot accordingly. Likewise, inform them if someone on their team is on a performance improvement plan, rather than letting them discover it on their own, as they will be quick to identify who is not performing and a heads up will prevent a shock to their system. Sharing knowledge will build trust and improve their ability to make an impact and establish authority.

Make the new hire aware of common challenges in your environment to avoid surprises.

Also, be prepared to let go of people who cannot keep up with the high level of performance that a rockstar brings and expects of others. As we know, this new hire is highly aligned with the organization's values and goals. And again, that can rock the boat with people who are "comfortable" coasting or underperforming.

Lastly, establish a formal feedback loop. Ideally, you should have an open-door policy for any urgent matters. If the feedback process in your organization is more formal, make sure the new person knows how to access or utilize it and how often it happens. Establishing that type of communication up front is tremendously helpful and can also benefit your organization through opportunities for growth and change.

When done right, onboarding is a collaborative effort. It includes everyone on the team, not just HR and talent acquisition teams. To be truly successful, you need buy-in from other leaders and colleagues. Show them how they will fit into the onboarding process and how the new hire will make their life better. As a result, they will greet the new team member with greater warmth, making them feel more connected and motivated.

Build a Leadership Pipeline

One of the most pressing and widespread challenges facing companies today is the shortage of ready leadership—individuals equipped to navigate compounding pressures, from accelerating AI advancements to increasing market uncertainty. When you invest in rockstars in your organization, you are actively building a strong and resilient leadership pipeline that will future proof your company.

As McKinsey researchers wrote in a 2024 essay on the future of leadership, "The organizations that treat leadership development as a core capability and proactively address the needs of both existing and aspiring leaders can raise their overall resilience and substantially improve the odds that they will be able to withstand disruption."[40] The most successful organizations do not recruit leaders, per se—rather, they identify high performers from the start, offer them opportunities for growth and advancement, and nurture them so the company can grow its own leaders.

Successful companies go to great lengths to hire the best talent. As Steve Jobs said, "The secret of my success is that we have gone to exceptional lengths to hire the best people in the world." And the *most* successful companies go to even greater lengths to retain high performers.

"The secret of my success is that we have gone to exceptional lengths to hire the best people in the world."

– Steve Jobs

Why? Because high performers are invaluable assets—when you invest in their growth and empower their upward trajectory, they deliver impact at every level of the organization. And your investment in them generates loyalty.

It may seem like a simple formula: as a high performer's career advances, so does their loyalty. And if they are loyal, they will not want to leave. That means attrition down, retention up. Most companies and leaders understand this, but they miss easy opportunities to instill that sense of loyalty.

What can you do to help your rockstar continuously improve and to help them get to the next level? Two best practices you can implement during onboarding (and beyond!) to create your own leadership pipeline are mentorship and recognition programs.

The Power of Mentorship

One key element of tailoring onboarding for rockstars is **formal mentorship**—a powerful opportunity that many companies overlook. If you want to retain a high performer, I strongly recommend assigning a mentor from day one. This demonstrates from the very beginning that you are investing in their growth and want to set them up for success. Every environment is different, and having a dedicated mentor will build trust quicker and more deeply. A mentor provides guidance, is a key point of contact for specific questions, serves as a sounding board for new ideas, and helps fast-track their ability to adapt to a new environment.

The evidence is clear: if you want to increase a high performer's job satisfaction, career progression, sense of belonging, and the success of their whole team, mentorship is non-negotiable. According to a Forbes contributor, "Nearly 70% of businesses reported an increase in productivity due to mentoring, and more than 50% say these programs had a positive impact on profits."[41]

Nearly 70% of businesses reported an increase in productivity due to mentoring, and more than 50% say these programs had a positive impact on profits.

A dedicated mentor can also boost employee retention and reduce attrition. Research by McKinsey shows that mentorship programs can improve retention rates by 35%, especially among high-potential employees.[42] McKinsey also found that employees who feel supported through mentorship are more engaged, loyal, and likely to stay longer with their organizations.[43]

Mentorship programs can improve retention rates by 35%.

Now, **mentorship will only work when the right party is involved**. Be sure to choose the right mentor. Of course, the mentor needs to be a high performer. Like attracts like. And ideally, the mentor should have some commonalities with the rockstar who just joined your team (just like we aligned interviewers with candidates based on commonalities to increase attraction in Chapter 3). It could be someone with a similar background or shared alma mater—or a mentor who started in the same role and has since advanced into the very position the new hire is being fast-tracked for. The mentor should also have at least three years of experience in your organization, so that they are fully versed in the culture and have experienced and overcome a variety of challenges. As we all know, the more time you spend with an organization, the more you will understand the best practices and the nuances that come with being successful within that specific organization.

Furthermore, all of the warmth built and momentum generated during the recruitment process should continue into the onboarding process—especially in those critical first 90 days. How? Be available and be proactive! It is genuinely as easy as saying "Let's check in," and following through. It could be once a week or once a month depending on the person and your own availability. But it is very important that the mentor-mentee relationship not be one-sided. Relationships are a two-way street. You as a leader set the tone and standards for what being a mentor means at your company.

Imagine a scenario where a recently hired high performer schedules time with their mentor, and their meeting is cancelled every time. That is a point of failure. It decreases the value of that relationship to the rockstar—and to your company. If a new hire is left to figure it out on their own, they may feel like they are being underutilized or underappreciated, and it may push them towards exploring other options. What I have seen is this: The *wrong* mentor will drive high performers away.

To avoid any breakdowns in the relationship, it is always a good idea to formally track the mentorship. How many touchpoints have there been in the first quarter? What were they about? What was the quality and duration of each check in? This builds accountability into the structure of mentor-mentee relationships.

A study by Deloitte found that, "Companies with a strong culture of mentoring report a 20% increase in innovation and adaptability to change."[44] So your investment does go a long way. As for your leadership pipeline, research shows that 75% of executives credit their success to mentors, and 90% of employees with a career mentor are happy at work."[45] Formal mentorships are powerful relationship builders and can be transformative for the longevity and success of your organization.

"75% of executives credit their success to mentors, and 90% of employees with a mentor are happy at work."

"Thank You" and Recognition Goes a Long Way to Building Loyalty

It is a basic principle of human psychology that we respond best to positive reinforcement. In the workplace, this translates into rewards and recognition. Where rewards are those tangible benefits we receive, such as bonuses and company perks, recognition comes in the form of gratitude and positive feedback. Of the two, recognition is a low cost, high-impact strategy, and it is easy to forget how vitally essential it is to employee productivity and satisfaction.

How do you feel when you are recognized for your achievements? It's an energizing, validating feeling—one that fuels even greater commitment and performance. A recent Gallup poll found that companies with strong recognition programs have 31% lower voluntary turnover rates.[46] That same survey found that nearly a quarter of employees reported that their most memorable recognition came from a CEO.[47]

Companies with strong recognition programs have 31% lower voluntary turnover rates.

Make it meaningful. Personalize it. And be thoughtful about who you choose to deliver the message of recognition. Most importantly, recognition is a means of showing that you *care* about them as a person. As we have discussed throughout the book, this rockstar is a person, not a product. It is important to treat them as such.

Furthermore, when you do recognize them for their achievements, connect the recognition back to the company's values for maximum impact. For example, if they have achieved a high-impact milestone, you might say, "The way you executed [this specific situation] truly reflected our values of [X, Y, Z]. It set a powerful example for all of us. Thank you for that."

By mentioning a situation, then tying it back to the company's values, they see the correlation between the impact of their contributions and the alignment they feel with the organization. And high performers *stay* when they feel appreciated. They put their heart and soul into what they do. If you want them to continue to be exceptional, to go above and beyond, recognition is a must.

*High performers **stay***
when they feel appreciated.

Once again, this practice is about moving away from the old transactional ways of doing business into more strategic methods. Having a strong, value-driven culture boosts employee motivation and engagement, increases productivity, and minimizes turnover.

In a survey of more than 16,000 professionals working in more than 4,000 organizations, from C-suite leaders to junior staff members, Deloitte found that 54% of employees prefer a verbal "Thank you" for their day-to-day accomplishments.[48] It may seem obvious, but it is an easy opportunity many of us miss. That same survey asked what managers could do that would motivate employees to produce great work, and the most frequent answer by far was "recognize me."[49] And when recognition aligns with company values, it reinforces purpose.

*When recognition aligns with company
values, it reinforces purpose.*

Values-based recognition programs have been shown to increase employee satisfaction by 86%[50], boost employee performance by an average of 11.1%[51], and organizations with strong recognition cultures are 12 times more likely to have successful business outcomes.[52] Those figures can translate to massive increases in efficiency and profound gains for your bottom line, not to mention the overall happiness of your workforce.

Recognize the actions that reflect the team's shared goals. Focus on those actions that align with shared vision in order to deepen employees' sense of belonging. As Richard Branson famously put it, "Train people well enough so they can leave. Treat them well enough so they don't want to." Recognition and a deeper sense of belonging will increase retention, loyalty, and career advancement.

*"Train people well enough so they can leave. Treat
them well enough so they don't want to."*

– Richard Branson

That last point is key. For high performers, the best reward is career progression. For more significant achievements, consider recognizing the rockstar's efforts with new opportunities for growth. Deloitte found that this was employees' preferred method of recognition (47%), even above salary increases (23%) and bonuses (10%).[53] When you recognize a high performer and give them credit as a leader, you empower them to do greater and greater things on behalf of your organization.

How to Minimize Burnout

While recognition is critical to retention, it's important to remember that even a rockstar has limits to the value they can contribute each day. Burnout is mental, emotional, and physical exhaustion from sustaining a high-stress, heavy workload over an extended period of time, and it is a serious problem not just for high-performing individuals but for organizations as a whole. Decades of research show that, in addition to the detrimental physical and mental health consequences, burnout can deeply damage organizations through employee absenteeism, job dissatisfaction, loss of productivity, increased attrition, and errors that lead to drops in service quality and even negative impacts on your bottom line.[54]

Thankfully, there are easy steps you can implement to prevent it from happening and keep the high performers you worked so hard to recruit happy, healthy, and productive.

The Magic of Mini-breaks
We all know that person in the office who prides themselves on being the first one in in the morning, eating lunch at their desk, and being the last to leave. They take on more and more responsibilities until they

hit the breaking point. It is an old-fashioned model of dedication—and the model is broken. We know from multiple studies that short breaks prevent burnout as well as long-term health problems.

As little as five- to ten-minute "mini-breaks" are enough to relieve overworked parts of the brain, refresh cognitive functioning, and increase the likelihood of achieving work goals.[55] It is reasonable to assume that high performers will be tasked with continuous, challenging, thought-provoking work, and mini-breaks are an easy, low-cost remedy for reducing stress, improving mental clarity, and boosting productivity. Plus, these same studies show improved morale, health, and happiness as a result.[56]

"Mini-breaks" relieve overworked parts of the brain, refresh cognitive functioning, and increase the likelihood of achieving work goals.

Avoiding burnout is about finding the right balance. A high performer will naturally be inclined to keep working. Their exceptional standards motivate them to continue adding value wherever they can. The more they exceed expectations, the more responsibilities they are given, and the more they feel the need to keep exceeding those expectations. But there has to be a reasonable limit. No one can maintain the pressure and exertion of working 24/7 on a hamster wheel. That type of stress has consequences, not just on the individual. Job-related stress costs companies hundreds of *billions* of dollars each year.[57]

Part of your role as a leader is creating the space and permission for high performers to prioritize their well-being. You set the tone. Be a vocal advocate of the mini-break, especially where it incorporates physical movement like getting up to stretch or walk. Display a one-pager in your office or breakroom highlighting the benefits of mini-breaks, and ensure new hires receive a copy as part of their onboarding. Emphasize that incorporating this into their daily routine at work will help them make better decisions, reduce errors, and boost their energy. Make it part of your "built" environment to increase retention.

This Meeting Could Have Been an Email

Another universal truth in today's office culture is the dreaded "meeting that could have been an email." When I was working in the corporate world, I remember one time being called into a meeting by my CEO. As I sat there listening to someone in a different department going on and on about matters that were unrelated to any of my projects or responsibilities, I thought, *What am I doing here? I could be at my desk making the company money right now.*

As ten minutes turned into twenty, I could not take it anymore. I stood up and said, "I'm going to excuse myself," and I left the meeting. I did not feel bad. Actually, it was invigorating. I knew I was not going to get fired or reprimanded because I was producing greater results than anyone else in that meeting, and the CEO knew that (as I was his second in command and he confided in me about the underperforming team members)—and I knew my priority was just that, getting results.

I think most of us have been in meetings where we wanted to get up and leave. It is a drain on our energy and resources. We have all been there, and yet, somehow this keeps happening! So, while this next piece of advice may seem straightforward, it is often missed. One of the easiest ways to reduce burnout and frustration among high performers is to be intentional about their time—starting with removing them from non-priority meetings. Choose which meetings they actually need to participate in based on the projects and strategic planning they are directly involved with. Then, let them focus on the goals that will increase your ROI and impact the whole team.

An easy way to avoid burnout and frustration for high performers is to simply be selective and not have them in non-priority meetings.

I also see my most successful clients leveraging AI to this end. With AI, you can generate meeting notes and a summary that high performers can digest in seconds, instead of wasting two hours of their time which would be better spent on high-value activities.

Rockstars are major assets and significant value drivers for your company. Ensure you are using their time and expertise wisely.

Pivot Like a Pro

The final point I want to make stems from a belief popularized by Gary Shapiro's bestseller, *Pivot or Die.*[58] As the CEO and Vice Chair of the Consumer Technology Association, Shapiro noticed a trend among the most resilient, successful, high-performing businesses: the ability of their leadership to **pivot**. He points to pioneering enterprises like Amazon, Netflix, and Google that disrupted the status quo in their respective industries—and made unparalleled profits because of their willingness to change course.

Knowing when to pivot applies to how you manage high performers, since retention sometimes means pivoting high performers within the organization. Once you get to know them on an even deeper level, have time to observe how they interact with others, and see the results they produce, you may identify that this high performer would add even more value if they were involved in a different area of the company.

High performers often bring a depth of knowledge and experience, which have the potential to be applied across multiple aspects of an organization. Use that broad skill set to your advantage, and pivot them to different areas of the business to maximize your return on investment!

So, remember, the first 90 days of onboarding are critical to making high performers feel confident in their choice to stay committed to your company. Reward that choice with a warm environment, a meaningful mentorship program, values-based recognition for their accomplishments, and work that energizes them and avoids burnout.

RITA'S INSIGHTS

- To maximize buy-in, make formal introductions with key contacts and leaders early on in the onboarding process. This helps new rockstars feel welcomed, connected, and reinforces the warmth built during recruitment.
- Assign a mentor based on commonalities, experience, and shared career trajectory. Track the quality and success of the mentor-mentee relationship. Remember, mentorship programs can improve retention rates by as much as 35%!
- Use recognition to acknowledge high performers' achievements and connect that recognition to your company's values. This is a powerful tool to motivate consistent results and increase retention.
- Reduce the risk of attrition by avoiding burnout. Encourage mini-breaks, avoid unnecessary meetings, and "pivot or die!"

CHAPTER 11

A FRAMEWORK FOR THE FUTURE

The Build–Engage–Close™ Framework is designed to solve talent recruitment challenges both now and in the future. It's about equipping yourself—today—for the leadership demands your organization will face as it continues to grow and evolve.

There will continue to be a shortage of great talent.

If you want to win the talent war, you must understand: **talent strategy *is* business strategy**.

As Bain & Company emphasizes, "Great talent is the foundation of great performance. Winning organizations treat talent as a strategic asset, not a functional necessity." The ability to attract high-performing professionals is *the* competitive advantage. It's what accelerates growth, and without the right people, your success is always going to be capped.

Talent strategy is business strategy.

When you focus on hiring rockstars, results will follow thanks to their agility, problem-solving ability, and relentless drive. They can increase momentum, grow your bottom line, improve camaraderie, and, frankly, make everything better. You simply have to be willing to invest—in the recruitment process and in the rockstars themselves— knowing that it's ultimately an investment in the long-term success of your business.

In this book, we went into depth on how the Build–Engage–Close Framework positions you to consistently attract rockstar talent while your competitors struggle with outdated, ineffective tactics.

In Part I, we looked at how to **build** a foundation based on the *law of attraction* and the importance of making sure you have the right *advocate*, *brand*, and *message* in place to create a *Rockstar Attraction Engine* that will keep momentum high and drive recruitment success. And we also uncovered how the wrong recruiter—or the wrong advocate—can cost you financially and do long-term damage to your brand and reputation. The *right strategic recruiter* will save you time, energy, *and* money by identifying gaps in your current talent acquisition strategy, leveraging their network to find the best aligned candidates, and applying best practices to optimize processes.

Then in Part II, we examined how to **engage** the right drivers for a successful outcome. This included applying innovative sales tactics and leading-edge research in human psychology to build meaningful *rapport*, find *alignment*, and emphasize *quality over quantity*.

We learned how critical it is to have the right *advocate* in place at each step, to ensure we don't repel the rockstar and to avoid common mistakes, including being too aggressive and pushy, treating the interview process as transactional, or being unable to ask deep questions and pivot conversations. We also discussed best practices for vetting and interviewing to help you identify true rockstars, along with strategies for keeping momentum high leading into the offer stage—where timing and alignment are often the deciding factors.

Lastly, in Part III, we reiterated that the **close** is happening incrementally in every interaction, but the final steps are the most sensitive. I shared the three most common mistakes organizations make during the offer stage—waiting too long to extend an offer, having the wrong person communicate an offer, and making too low an offer. We also learned that often, it is a *very small detail that causes a deal to fall apart*. The same is true for negotiations: *who* you use to negotiate for your company directly impacts the outcome. Make sure it is someone who knows how to *pivot*, deeply understands the candidate's goals, and will represent your best interests. All of which highlights the immense value of a *strategic recruiting partner* who has the *gut instinct* and experience to apply and master all the nuances of my Build–Engage–Close Framework.

This framework has been fine-tuned through years of hands-on experience with fast-moving, results-driven organizations. Even if you implement just one or two small strategies from the book, I am confident you will see positive outcomes.

Your advocate in the process,
whether internal or external, can make or break
the Build–Engage–Close Framework.

However, it takes nailing all of the nuances of each of the three elements at every single stage in the recruitment process to find and close a rockstar. **Your advocate in the process, whether internal or external, can make or break the Build–Engage–Close Framework**. That is because every detail in every interaction matters.

Every organization has gaps in their recruitment process. Whether it is missing a component of the Rockstar Attraction Engine, having the wrong person interview a rockstar, or mishandling the timing during the offer and negotiation stage. Having read the book, the Build–Engage–Close Framework may have already helped you identify some of those gaps—giving you the insight needed to fully optimize your talent strategy. Because leveraging the right strategy is everything when it comes to securing rockstars.

You have come to fully grasp the critical importance and complexity of the *right* strategy at the heart of strategic recruiting. It is not enough to throw spaghetti at the wall and hope that something sticks as a quantity over quality approach never leads to the most successful outcomes.

It is not transactional recruitment that wins the talent war. It is strategic recruitment.

The leaders and organizations that will win in the long run are those that use a proven system—the Build–Engage–Close Framework— to consistently attract, vet, and retain rockstars with the power to transform your business. If you are not seeing the results you want, it could be time to engage a strategic recruiter that knows how to get every detail right.

It is not transactional recruitment
that wins the talent war.
It is strategic recruitment.

Action, Execution, and Results

Selective Insight partnered with a global advisory firm in the San Francisco Bay area to recruit a seasoned professional to lead their team. I helped them secure a rockstar, a female leader whose leadership, excellence, and vision would ignite the team's next level of growth.

Just recently, she got in touch to tell me how things were going (again, this is what rapport and relationship building looks like when it is done right!).

"I just had my performance review," she told me. "And I received confirmation that they have made me an equity partner in the firm."

"That is fantastic. Great work and congratulations," I said. "That is a huge deal to reach partner in such a short period of time."

And she earned it. In a super competitive market, she helped grow the company's client base by 3x and increased their bottom line by 30%. The company has also seen an increase in retention, thanks to this rockstar being a great mentor to other team members, which is helping the company develop their own leadership pipeline and retain their best talent longer.

Having a rockstar on your team creates a multiplier effect. One success builds on the next, driving continuous growth and compounding results.

Having a rockstar on your team creates a *multiplier* effect. One success builds on the next, driving continuous growth and compounding results.

Stories like this are the reason I do what I do. We get to see the success of companies and candidates for *years*. It's incredibly rewarding to witness their growth and to contribute to the transformation of both the organization and its leaders. It's a privilege to align high-performing talent with high-performing organizations—those striving for excellence, reshaping industries, and driving meaningful impact in the marketplace. That passion fuels our purpose. It is those success stories that I get to share with my daughter at the end of the day and tell her, "Guess what Mommy did today? Mommy found a rockstar!"

The intention behind building a true strategic partnership is to make other people's lives easier and better and to make their companies more successful. I love to hear back from clients, "You are a lifesaver." A strategic partner is someone who knows your vision and culture and who can articulate it in the right manner to candidates who are highly aligned. No more dealing with hundreds of resumes, conducting dozens of interviews, only to lose your top-choice candidate to a competitor—because alignment wasn't established from the start. No.

With a strategic recruiter, you get three quality candidates who are all aligned and eager to deliver real ROI. There is a better way. Take it!

We all know trust in business is hard to come by. But the results will speak for themselves. Our track record of consistent proven results speaks to the effectiveness of the Build–Engage–Close Framework and the undeniable value of a strategic recruiting partner.

As one client of ours shared in her testimonial: "Rita makes the effort to truly understand what we are looking for. She looks beyond experiences and credentials to find the right skill set and growth potential. Equally important, Rita looks out for her candidates. She takes the time to learn our company and our culture and what makes us attractive for the right person. She represents our company very well with candidates. Rita operates with transparency. She values long-term relationships and has both employer's and candidate's long-term interest in mind."

Having looked under the hood of multiple organizations, excellence has become easy to recognize. You can put a rusty Pontiac engine into a Ferrari, but it's still going to run like a rusty old Pontiac. The key is getting under the hood and looking at the smallest details, yet you have to know where to look and what you are looking for. Accurately spotting rockstar talent, building rapport, and assessing alignment comes from deep, hands-on experience. If you want a lineup of high-powered, high-performing Ferraris—an organization supercharged by rockstar talent—it is time to take the next action step to optimize your recruitment strategy.

FINAL INSIGHTS

This book was written to shed light on the overlooked details and provide fresh perspectives on strategic recruitment. The insights and approaches shared are meant to challenge how you think about talent and help drive meaningful, measurable growth in your organization.

The Build–Engage–Close Framework is here to inspire action. It's built to help you attract and retain high performers with confidence and clarity.

After all, *one* rockstar outweighs twenty average performers—every single time—when it comes to real ROI and exponential growth.

Finally, I want to thank you for reading my book, for your time and trust. Exceptional teams aren't built by chance, they're built by intention.

The next step is simple: leverage the right strategic recruiter to help implement the Build–Engage–Close Framework in your organization. Because hiring isn't just a process. It's the strategy that decides who wins the talent war.

YOU'RE ONE
ROCKSTAR AWAY

Hiring shouldn't be the hardest part of growth.

The right talent brings clarity, momentum, and transformation.

It should make leadership easier, not harder.

What slows progress isn't effort. It's complexity, misalignment, and too many average candidates.

What accelerates it? Rockstars. Precision. A strategy that works.

The organizations that win are led by those who hire with intention— leaders who understand that the right talent isn't just a hire, it's a *multiplier.*

If you're committed to finding your next multiplier, I'd love to help.

Reach out to me directly: rbaroody@selectiveinsight.com

Warmly,
Rita

ABOUT THE AUTHOR

Rita Baroody is the CEO and Co-Founder of Selective Insight, a national recruiting firm that partners with growth organizations to attract, secure, and retain high-performing professionals. Rita has helped companies generate hundreds of millions in increased valuations by hiring the right talent.

With her experience as a top-performing executive recruiter, talent strategist, and former CPA, she partners with growth-minded leaders to help them make smarter, more strategic hiring decisions.

Rita's Build–Engage–Close™ Framework brings clarity to a complex hiring landscape—and has been proven to consistently attract, close, and retain rockstars.

Rita is passionate about helping growth-minded leaders build high-performing teams and strongly believes that alignment of values, goals, and skills is critical to long-term success.

When she's not advising leaders, Rita enjoys time by the water with her husband and daughter.

Connect with her on LinkedIn and YouTube @RitaBaroody.

ENDNOTES

1   Noguera Lasa, A. et al. "In the spotlight: Performance management that puts people first." McKinsey & Company. https://www.mckinsey.com/capabilities/people-and-organizational-performance/our-insights/in-the-spotlight-performance-management-that-puts-people-first

2   Keller, S. "Attracting and retaining the right talent." McKinsey & Company. 24 November 2017. https://www.mckinsey.com/capabilities/people-and-organizational-performance/our-insights/attracting-and-retaining-the-right-talent

3   Ibid.

4   Thims, Libb. (2007). Human Chemistry (Volume Two). Morrisville, NC: LuLu, p. 378.

5   West, A., et al. "Achieving growth: Putting leadership mindsets and behaviors into action." McKinsey Quarterly. 13 January 2025. https://www.mckinsey.com/capabilities/growth-marketing-and-sales/our-insights/achieving-growth-putting-leadership-mindsets-and-behaviors-into-action

6   Ibid.

7   Devalekar, Ashish. "Growth Mindset: How Companies Get To The Next Level In The Digital World." Forbes. 21 April 2022. https://www.forbes.com/councils/forbesbusinesscouncil/2021/11/12/growth-mindset-how-companies-get-to-the-next-level-in-the-digital-world/

8   Ibid.

9   Bellet, C., De Neve, J.E., and Ward, G. "Does Employee Happiness have an Impact on Productivity?" Saïd Business School. 14 October 2019. http://dx.doi.org/10.2139/ssrn.3470734

10 Moss, J. "Creating a Happier Workplace Is Possible — and Worth It." Harvard Business Review. 20 October 2023. https://hbr.org/2023/10/creating-a-happier-workplace-is-possible-and-worth-it

11 Chamorro-Premuzic, T. and Kirschner, J. "How the Best Managers Identify and Develop Talent." Harvard Business Review. 9 January

2020. https://hbr.org/2020/01/how-the-best-managers-identify-and-develop-talent?registration=success

12 Cloke, H. "Dweck's Mindset Theory: How to Develop a Growth Mindset." Growth Engineering. 12 March 2025. https://www.growthengineering.co.uk/growth-mindset/

13 Robinson, B., PhD. "80% Of Companies Say A Growth Mindset Among Employees Directly Drives Profits." Forbes. 27 Oct. 2024. https://www.forbes.com/sites/bryanrobinson/2024/10/27/80-of-companies-say-a-growth-mindset-among-employees-directly-drives-profits/

14 Ibid.

15 Cloke, H. "Dweck's Mindset Theory: How to Develop a Growth Mindset." Growth Engineering. 12 March 2025. https://www.growthengineering.co.uk/growth-mindset/

16 Rampl LV & Kenning P. "Employer brand trust and affect: linking brand personality to employer brand attractiveness." European Journal of Marketing. 2014. 48:218–36. DOI:10.1108/EJM-02-2012-0113

17 Percy, S. "Ask The Right Questions: Why You Should Enable Your Team To Challenge." Forbes. 31 Aug. 2024. https://www.forbes.com/sites/sallypercy/2024/08/31/ask-the-right-questions-why-you-should-enable-your-team-to-challenge/

18 Lievens, Filip & Slaughter, Jerel. "Employer Image and Employer Branding: What We Know and What We Need to Know." Annual Review of Organizational Psychology and Organizational Behavior. 2016 (3). 10.1146/annurev-orgpsych-041015-062501.

19 Fatemi, F. "The True Cost of a Bad Hire—It's More Than You Think." Forbes. 28 Sept. 2016. https://www.forbes.com/sites/falonfatemi/2016/09/28/the-true-cost-of-a-bad-hire-its-more-than-you-think/

20 Ibid.

21 Chapman, D., et al. (2005). "Applicant Attraction to Organizations and Job Choice: A Meta-Analytic Review of the Correlates of Recruiting Outcomes." The Journal of applied psychology. 90. 928-44. 10.1037/0021-9010.90.5.928.

22 Ibid.

23 Ibid.

24 Zhao, X. and Epley, N. "Insufficiently complimentary?: Underestimating the positive impact of compliments creates a barrier to expressing them." Journal of Personality and Social Psychology. Aug 2021, 121(2): 239-256. https://doi.org/10.1037/pspa0000277

25 Billsberry, J., et al. "Towards a composite map of organisational person–environment fit." (2000). British Academy of Management Annual Conference, Oxford. https://www.academia.edu/46963639/ Towards_a_composite_map_of_organisational_person_ environment_fit1

26 Freedman, M., supra.

27 Lievens, Filip & Slaughter, Jerel. "Employer Image and Employer Branding: What We Know and What We Need to Know." Annual Review of Organizational Psychology and Organizational Behavior. 2016 (3). 10.1146/annurev-orgpsych-041015-062501

28 Pritlove, C., et al. "The good, the bad, and the ugly of implicit bias." The Lancet. Vol. 393 (10171): 502 – 504. https://www.thelancet.com/ journals/lancet/article/PIIS0140-6736(18)32267-0/fulltext

29 Caren, A. "Why we often remember the bad better than the good." The Washington Post. 1 Nov. 2018. https://www.washingtonpost. com/science/2018/11/01/why-we-often-remember-bad-better-than-good/?noredirect=on

30 Becker, W., et al. "The Effect of Job Offer Timing on Offer Acceptance, Performance, and Turnover." Personnel Psychology. Spring 2010; 63(1): 223-241, p. 223. https://doi.org/10.1111/j.1744-6570.2009.01167.x

31 Walker, H.J., et al. "Is This How I Will Be Treated? Reducing Uncertainty through Recruitment Interactions." Academy of Management Journal.19 July 2012; 56(5). https://doi.org/10.5465/ amj.2011.0196

32 Voss, Chris. Never Split the Difference: Negotiating as If Your Life Depended on It. Random House: 2016.

33 Ferguson, M., et al. "The Lingering Effects of the Recruitment Experience on the Long-Term Employment Relationship." Negotiation and Conflict Management Research. August 2008, 1(3): 246-262. https://doi.org/10.1111/j.1750-4716.2008.00015.x

34 Ibid.

35 Extejt, M.M. and Russell, C.J. "The Role of Individual Bargaining Behavior in the Pay Setting Process: A Pilot Study." Journal of Business

and Psychology. Fall 1990, 5(1): 113-126. http://www.jstor.org/stable/25092268?origin=JSTOR-pdf

36   Sass, M. and Liao-Troth, M. "Personality and Negotiation Performance: The People Matter" Journal of Collective Negotiations. 18 Jan. 2015. http://dx.doi.org/10.2139/ssrn.2549992

37   Voss, Chris. Never Split the Difference: Negotiating as If Your Life Depended on It. Random House: 2016.

38   Rau, B., and Feinauer, D. "The role of internal agents in starting salary negotiations." Human Resource Management Review. 2006, 16(1):47-66. https://doi.org/10.1016/j.hrmr.2006.02.002.

39   Voss, Chris. Never Split the Difference: Negotiating as If Your Life Depended on It. Random House: 2016.

40   Sternfels, B., et al. "The art of 21st-century leadership: From succession planning to building a leadership factory." McKinsey. 22 Oct. 2024. https://www.mckinsey.com/capabilities/strategy-and-corporate-finance/our-insights/the-art-of-21st-century-leadership-from-succession-planning-to-building-a-leadership-factory

41   Reeves, M. "6 Benefits Of Mentoring In The 2023 Workplace." Forbes. 6 Oct. 2023. https://www.forbes.com/councils/forbeshumanresourcescouncil/2023/10/06/6-benefits-of-mentoring-in-the-2023-workplace/

42   "The Value of Mentoring: Proven Benefits and Data-Driven Insights." LinkedIn. 18 Aug. 2024. https://www.linkedin.com/pulse/value-mentoring-proven-benefits-data-driven-insights-d2wtf/

43   Ibid.

44   Ibid.

45   Gross, C.J. "A Better Approach to Mentorship." Harvard Business Review. 6 June 2023. https://hbr.org/2023/06/a-better-approach-to-mentorship

46   Gallup. (2016). Employee recognition: Low cost, high impact. https://www.gallup.com/workplace/236441/employee-recognition-low-cost-high-impact.aspx

47   Ibid.

48   "The Practical Magic of 'Thank You': How your people want to be recognized, for what, and by whom." Deloitte. June 2019. https://www2.deloitte.com/content/dam/Deloitte/us/Documents/about-deloitte/us-about-deloitte-the-practical-magic-of-thank-you-june-2019.pdf

49 Ibid.

50 "The power of recognition programs for employee engagement." HRD Connect. 24 May 2024. https://www.hrdconnect.com/2024/05/24/the-power-of-recognition-programs-for-employee-engagement/

51 Motivosity. (n.d.). Rewards & recognition program. https://www.motivosity.com/blog/rewards-recognition-program/

52 Bersin, J. "New research unlocks the secret of employee recognition." Forbes. 2012. https://www.forbes.com/sites/joshbersin/2012/06/13/new-research-unlocks-the-secret-of-employee-recognition/

53 "The Practical Magic of 'Thank You': How your people want to be recognized, for what, and by whom." Deloitte. June 2019. https://www2.deloitte.com/content/dam/Deloitte/us/Documents/about-deloitte/us-about-deloitte-the-practical-magic-of-thank-you-june-2019.pdf

54 "Employers need to focus on workplace burnout: Here's why." American Psychological Association.12 May 2023. https://www.apa.org/topics/healthy-workplaces/workplace-burnout

55 Brooks, C. "The Key to Increasing Productivity? Employee Breaks."

Business News Daily. 22 Aug. 2024. https://www.businessnewsdaily.com/6387-employee-breaks.html

56 Ibid.

57 Ibid.

58 Shapiro, Gary. Pivot or Die: How Leaders Thrive When Everything Changes. William Morrow: 2024.

.